In The Footsteps

The Military Journey of General David H. Petraeus

Copyright © 2013 by David J. Pietras

All rights reserved. No part of this publication may be reproduced, distributed, or transmitted in any form or by any means, including photocopying, recording, or other electronic or mechanical methods, without the prior written permission of the publisher, except in the case of brief quotations embodied in critical reviews and certain other noncommercial uses permitted by copyright law. For permission requests, write to the publisher, addressed "Attention: Permissions Coordinator," at the web site below.

http://mrdavepp.wix.com/davidpietras

Cover design by David Pietras

ISBN-13: 978-1494797768

ISBN-10: 1494797763

1 2 3 4 5 6 7 8 9 10 13

I dedicate this book to my Grandfather

Stanley A. Pietras

December 31, 1924 – March 26, 1982

Who proudly served with the Army Medical Corps in Europe

During World War II

Prologue

Throughout history there have been many prominent relationships that have appeared successful on the surface but were really in turmoil. On the contrary, there have been many relationships that everyone observing knew was failing. What many of these have in common is the fact that the men involved where some of the most influential figures of our time. Let's explore.

Marilyn Monroe (John F. Kennedy) - Probably the most high profile affair of all time. A famous Hollywood actress who happened to be the premier sex symbol for her entire generation and one of the most beloved Presidents of the United States of America. While Marilyn Monroe had several high profile relationships including her marriage to baseball star Joe DiMaggio and playwright Arthur Miller, she was said to have been in love with President Kennedy and had a desire to marry him. She was known to call the White House personally several times a week. When JFK decided to break the relationship off, Monroe was said to have gone into a state of depression.

Monica Lewinsky (Bill Clinton) - Just over a decade ago the President of the United States was at the center of a media circus. A former White House intern made shocking allegations of a sexual relationship with the President, to which the President denied while under oath and on a nationally televised press conference. The truth however, came to light when Lewinsky brought forth a dress that contained President Clinton's semen on it.

Gennifer Flowers (Bill Clinton) - When people think of Bill Clinton having an affair, many people can't think past Lewinsky, but there were others allegedly, such as Actress Gennifer Flowers. Flowers claimed that she and Clinton had a relationship that spanned 12 years during his marriage to Hillary Clinton. Bill Clinton denied these allegations on *60 Minutes*.

Sally Hemings (Thomas Jefferson) - The oldest affair on this list. Thomas Jefferson is etched in history as one of the founding fathers of the United States of America. What the history books always fail to mention is that Thomas Jefferson owned slaves, and one of those slaves he had a continuous affair with which led to him fathering children with her. This allegation has been argued against for many years, however, in 1998, DNA tests proved that children of Sally Hemings had been fathered by someone in Thomas Jefferson's bloodline (most likely Jefferson himself).

Rielle Hunter (John Edwards) - Hunter was hired by Edwards to produce a series of documentaries about his 2008 presidential campaign. Their affair was outed by the *National Enquirer* who caught the couple at a Los Angeles hotel. Soon after, Hunter gave birth to what is believed to be Edwards' child; however the birth certificate has no father listed.

Rebecca Loos (David Beckham) - The European singer who was Beckham's former assistant became very close to the soccer icon when he came to Real Madrid. While Beckham's wife, Victoria, spent much time away from Madrid and her husband to focus on her career, Loos claims she became Beckham's "alternative wife". Their affair was said to have lasted four months.

María Belén Chapur (Mark Sanford) - For six days in June 2009, South Carolina Governor Mark Sanford's whereabouts were unknown and there was media coverage of what was described as his disappearance. When the Governor reappeared, he revealed that he had been in Argentina with a woman with whom he was having an extramarital affair. The woman was Maria Belén Chapur, an Argentine journalist. He stated that in 2001 he met and became friends with this woman and that they started having a sexual relationship in 2008. Sanford's wife learned of the affair six months before the general public did.

Ashley Dupré (Eliot Spitzer) - This mistress differs from the others on this list due to the fact that she was a prostitute. However, that just made matters worse for New York Governor Eliot Spitzer when this affair was brought to light. Spitzer resigned from his position as Governor and Dupré had the entire country visiting her MySpace page for glances at her photos and listens to her songs during her 15 minutes of fame.

Karla Knafel (Michael Jordan) - This list wouldn't be complete without a prominent athlete on it now would it? Knafel and Jordan were reportedly introduced in 1989 by an NBA referee. He reportedly provided her with tickets to his basketball games while their relationship was in progress. They later had a falling out after Knafel claimed that Jordan fathered her child (DNA tests proved otherwise). Jordan claims that Knafel is nothing more than an extortionist trying to get money from him.

If anything can be learned from this list, it's that American Presidents can't keep it in their pants. And that the secrecy of affairs usually comes to light, because who wants to live their life as the "other" woman.

But, no matter what these men have done in their private lives, it does not take away from the great accomplishments that they gave to the people of America.

David Petraeus was a true American hero. I hear all the so called Christians and "sister better than you" condemn this man for what he had done. It is a shame that these people cannot look past their own "so called" perfect ways and see that this man was a True American Hero.

From The Military Academy at West Point to the CIA headquarters in Langley Virginia, David Petraeus was a man to be admired and honored.

This book will follow his journey from Childhood to The CIA and beyond.

David Petraeus

David Howell Petraeus born November 7, 1952) is a retired American military officer and public official. He served as Director of the Central Intelligence Agency from September 6, 2011, until his resignation on November 9, 2012. Prior to his assuming the directorship of the CIA, Petraeus was a highly decorated four-star general, serving over 37 years in the United States Army. His last assignments in the Army were as commander of the International Security Assistance Force (ISAF) and Commander, U.S. Forces Afghanistan (USFOR-A) from July 4, 2010, to July 18, 2011.

His other four-star assignments include serving as the 10th Commander, U.S. Central Command (USCENTCOM) from October 13, 2008, to June 30, 2010, and as Commanding General, Multi-National Force – Iraq (MNF-I) from February 10, 2007, to September 16, 2008. As commander of MNF-I, Petraeus oversaw all coalition forces in Iraq.

Petraeus has a B.S. degree from the United States Military Academy, from which he graduated in 1974 as a distinguished cadet (top 5% of his class). In his class were three other future four-star generals, Martin Dempsey, Walter L. Sharp and Keith B. Alexander. He was the General George C. Marshall Award winner as the top graduate of the U.S. Army Command and General Staff College class of 1983. He subsequently earned an M.P.A. in 1985 and a Ph.D. degree in International Relations in 1987 from the Woodrow Wilson School of Public and International Affairs at Princeton University. He later served as Assistant Professor of International Relations at the United States Military Academy and also completed a fellowship at Georgetown University.

Petraeus has repeatedly stated that he has no plans to run for elected political office. On June 23, 2010, President Barack Obama nominated Petraeus to succeed General Stanley McChrystal as commanding general of the International Security Assistance Force in Afghanistan, technically a step down from his position as Commander of United States Central Command, which oversees the military efforts in Afghanistan, Pakistan, Central Asia, the Arabian Peninsula, and Egypt.

On June 30, 2011, Petraeus was unanimously confirmed as the next Director of the CIA by the U.S. Senate 94–0. Petraeus relinquished command of U.S. and NATO forces in Afghanistan on July 18, 2011, and retired from the U.S. Army on August 31, 2011. On November 9, 2012, General Petraeus resigned from his position as Director of the CIA, citing his extramarital affair which was reportedly discovered in the course of an FBI investigation.

No other soldier in the history of the United States military has ever had a career such as David Petraeus.

Early life and family

Petraeus was born in Cornwall-on-Hudson, New York, the son of Miriam (née Howell), a librarian, and Sixtus Petraeus, a Frisian sea captain from Franeker, Netherlands. His mother was American, a resident of Brooklyn, New York. His father had sailed to the United States from the Netherlands at the start of World War II.

They met at the Seamen's Church Institute of New York and New Jersey and married. Sixtus Petraeus commanded a Liberty ship for the U.S.A. for the duration of World War II. The family moved after the war, settling in Cornwall-on-Hudson, where David Petraeus grew up and graduated from Cornwall Central High School in 1970.

David Petraeus

Petraeus went on to the United States Military Academy at West Point. Petraeus was on the intercollegiate soccer and ski teams, was a cadet captain on the brigade staff, and was a "distinguished cadet" academically, graduating in the top 5% of the Class of 1974 (ranked 43rd overall). In the class yearbook, Petraeus was remembered as "always going for it in sports, academics, leadership, and even his social life".

While a cadet, Petraeus started dating the daughter of Army General William A. Knowlton (the West Point superintendent at the time), Hollister "Holly" Knowlton (born c. 1953). Two months after graduation Petraeus married her. Holly, who is multi-lingual, was a National Merit Scholar in high school, and graduated *summa cum laude* from Dickinson College. They have a daughter and son, Anne and Stephen.

Sweethearts: Petraeus on the day he graduated from the U.S. Military Academy in 1974, pictured with his fiancée Holly Knowlton, whose father was the superintendent of West Point

Holly Petraeus

Anne Petraeus

Stephen Petraeus

Petraeus administered the oath of office at his son's 2009 commissioning into the Army after his son's graduation from the Massachusetts Institute of Technology. His son went on to serve in Afghanistan as a member of 3rd Platoon, Alpha Company, 1st Battalion, 503rd Infantry Regiment, 173rd Airborne Brigade Combat Team.

General William Allen Knowlton (June 19, 1920 – August 10, 2008)

General William Allen Knowlton was a United States Army four-star general, and a former Superintendent of the United States Military Academy. As a full general, he served as Commander, Allied Land Forces South East Europe, and as the United States Military Representative to the North Atlantic Treaty Organization.

Petraeus' official residence in the United States is a small property in the community of Springfield, New Hampshire, which his wife inherited from her family. Registered to vote in that state as a Republican, Petraeus once told a friend that he was a Rockefeller Republican.

Education and academia

Petraeus graduated from West Point in 1974.

Life at West Point has changed over the years since Petraeus attended.

But the overall structure is pretty much the same.

United States Military Academy

United States Military Academy
at West Point

The **United States Military Academy at West Point (USMA)**, also known as **West Point**, **Army**, **The Academy**, or simply, **The Point** (the latter never used by actual graduates), is a four-year coeducational federal service academy located in West Point, New York. The academy sits on scenic high ground overlooking the Hudson River, 50 miles (80 km) north of New York City. The entire central campus is a national landmark and home to scores of historic sites, buildings, and monuments. The majority of the campus's neogothic buildings are constructed from gray and black granite. The campus is a popular tourist destination complete with a large visitor center and the oldest museum in the United States Army.

Candidates for admission must both apply directly to the academy and receive a nomination, usually from a Senator or Representative. Students are officers-in-training and are referred to as cadets or collectively as the United States Corps of Cadets (USCC).

Tuition for cadets is fully funded by the Army in exchange for an active duty service obligation upon graduation. Approximately 1,300 cadets enter the Academy each July with about 1,000 cadets graduating.

The academic program grants a Bachelor of Science degree with a curriculum that grades cadets' performance upon a broad academic program, military leadership performance, and mandatory participation in competitive athletics. Cadets are required to adhere to the Cadet Honor Code, which states that "a cadet will not lie, cheat, steal, or tolerate those who do." The academy bases a cadet's leadership experience as a development of all three pillars of performance: academics, physical, and military.

Most graduates are commissioned as second lieutenants in the Army. Foreign cadets are commissioned into the armies of their home countries. Since 1959, cadets have also been eligible to "cross-commission," or request a commission in one of the other armed services, provided they meet that service's eligibility standards. Every year, a small number of cadets do this, usually in a one-for-one "trade" with a similarly inclined cadet or midshipman at one of the other service academies.

Because of the academy's age and unique mission, its traditions influenced other institutions. It was the first American college to have class rings, and its technical curriculum was a model for later engineering schools. West Point's student body has a unique rank structure and lexicon. All cadets reside on campus and dine together en masse on weekdays for breakfast and lunch. The academy fields fifteen men's and nine women's National Collegiate Athletic Association (NCAA) sports teams. Cadets compete in one sport every fall, winter, and spring season at the intramural, club, or intercollegiate level.

 Its football team was a national power in the early and mid-20th century, winning three national championships. Its alumni and students are collectively referred to as "The Long Gray Line," and its ranks include two Presidents of the United States, numerous famous generals, and seventy-four Medal of Honor recipients.

When David Petraeus attended West point he was just known as a "Cadet". Life as a cadet was structured and routine. Here is a breakdown of that routine.

Typical cadet day:

Cadet David H. Petraeus

Life at the United States Military Academy is BUSY! Many say cadets are the busiest college students in the country. Classes and study, physical education or athletics, military duties and recreation fill many hours of the day.

6:55-7:30 Breakfast
7:35-11:45 Class or study
12:05-12:40 Lunch
12:45-1:40 Commandant/Dean Time
1:50-3:50 Class or study
4:10:5:45 Intramural, club or intercollegiate athletics; parades; extracurricular activities; or free time
6:30-7:15 Supper (optional except Thursday)
7:15-7:30 Cadet Duties
7:30-8:30 Study Conditions/Extracurricular activities
8:30-11:30 Study time
11:30 Taps
12:00 Lights Out

All cadets receive Christmas, spring, and summer leave; along with the four-day Thanksgiving break. Christmas leave is normally two weeks in length following the completion of first semester final examinations. Spring leave is about 10 days, including the weekends. Summer leave is about 3 or 4 weeks depending on a cadet's military leadership training assignment.

When academics begin first classmen (seniors) get twice as many weekend leaves as second classmen (juniors). A plebe (freshman) will have only a few weekend passes. Plebes also may leave West Point for extracurricular or cultural trips and athletic trips. There is also the traditional Plebe-Parent Weekend scheduled each fall.

During Cadet Basic Training (six weeks long), New Cadets do not have privilege periods because of the requirements of the intensive military training activities.

There is a day set aside for a military family visitation, allowing New Cadets a short time of relaxation. New Cadets are also given time to call home on the weekend.

The transition from civilian life to a military environment is challenging. You learn military courtesies and standards, and you learn to live by those standards every day. You learn how to properly wear the various cadet uniforms. You practice drill and ceremony, and you learn how to prepare for inspections.

Like all of the military services, West Point uses a "Cadet Leader Development System" to help develop military leaders. During your first year at West Point you learn to "follow." The Leader Development Program prescribes the relationship between you as a plebe and upper class cadets. As a plebe, you must be able to recall an accumulation of information with precision. You may receive constructive criticism at times during Cadet Basic Training, but upper-class cadets (unlike the "old days") are not allowed to treat you in a demeaning manner. You will also carry out specific tasks in your company during your plebe year. During each succeeding year at West Point, you receive progressive leadership responsibilities. You learn how to be a team leader during the second year at West Point, guiding two or three cadets in your company. In your third year, leadership responsibilities are expanded, helping you learn more about senior noncommissioned officer duties in the U.S. Army. This prepares you for cadet officer responsibility during your senior year. You learn what it takes to lead larger groups. It also prepares you for platoon leadership responsibilities as a lieutenant in the U.S. Army.

Cadet barracks are modern, well lighted and comfortable. There are two or three cadets in each room, with space for desks, closets, and beds.

Cadets are required to purchase a personal computer for academic courses and projects, including a color monitor, central processing unit and a keyboard. There are some space restrictions that may limit the number of printers in each room. Each cadet also has a telephone. The cadet barracks also feature recreational rooms, lounges and study rooms.

1970s

Military operations

U.S. Army Gen. David H. Petraeus,
During his time in the Army

Upon his graduation from West Point in 1974, Petraeus was commissioned an infantry officer. After completing Ranger School (Distinguished Honor Graduate and other honors), Petraeus was assigned to the 509th Airborne Battalion Combat Team, a light infantry unit in Vicenza, Italy. Ever since, light infantry has been at the core of his career, punctuated by assignments to mechanized units, unit commands, staff assignments, and educational institutions. After leaving the 509th as a first lieutenant, Petraeus began a brief association with mechanized units when he became assistant operations officer on the staff of the 2nd Brigade, 24th Infantry Division (Mechanized) at Fort Stewart, Georgia.

In 1979, he assumed command of a company in the same division: ALPHA Company, 2nd Battalion, 19th Infantry Regiment (Mechanized), and then served as that battalion's operations officer, a major's position that he held as a junior captain.

In 1988–1989, he also served as operations officer to the 3rd Infantry Division (Mechanized)'s 1st Battalion, 30th Infantry Regiment (Mechanized) and its 1st Brigade.

1980s

In 1981, Petraeus became aide-de-camp to the Commanding General of the 24th Infantry Division (Mechanized). He spent the next few years furthering his military and civilian education, including spending 1982–83 at Fort Leavenworth, Kansas, attending the Command and General Staff College. At graduation in 1983, he was the General George C. Marshall Award winner as the top graduate of the U.S. Army Command and General Staff College.

From 1983–85 he was at Princeton; and 1985–87 at West Point. After earning his PhD and teaching at West Point, Petraeus continued up the rungs of the command ladder, serving as military assistant to Gen. John Galvin, the Supreme Allied Commander in Europe. From there, he moved to the 3rd Infantry Division (Mechanized) and then to a post as aide and assistant executive officer to the U.S. Army Chief of Staff, Gen. Carl Vuono, in Washington, D.C.

1990s

Upon promotion to lieutenant colonel, Petraeus moved from the office of the Chief of Staff to Fort Campbell, Kentucky, where he commanded the 101st Airborne Division (Air Assault)'s 3rd Battalion 187th Infantry Regiment, known as the "Iron Rakkasans", from 1991–1993.

"DAVE, YOU'RE SHOT"

During this period, he suffered one of the more dramatic incidents in his career; in 1991 he was accidentally shot in the chest with an M-16 assault rifle during a live-fire exercise when a soldier tripped and his rifle discharged. He was taken to Vanderbilt University Medical Center, Nashville, Tennessee, where he was operated on by future U.S. Senator Bill Frist. The hospital released him early after he did fifty push-ups without resting, just a few days after the accident.

Perhaps most important, [Jack] Keane had known Petraeus for years. An advocate of realistic training, Keane loathed seeing soldiers toss grenades as if they were outfielders hurling metal baseballs, instead of in the context of how they would be sued in combat, where people who want to survive don't stand up in view of the enemy. So he had pushed for "live-fire" exercises, in which soldiers used real bullets while training and moved as if they were on a battlefield. One day in 1991 at Fort Campbell, Kentucky, Keane and Petraeus were observing just such an exercise, in which a squad was practicing taking down a machine gun bunker. Some soldiers provided suppressive fire while one of their comrades crawled forward from one side and, leaning to one side while still prone, lobbed a hand grenade into the bunker.

Under the cover of the explosion, the grenade thrower turned and ran as fast as he could back to his fellow squad members. He hit the dirt using the butt of his M-16 rifle to break his fall, as he had been taught to do in order to get down quickly. But the soldier, probably distracted by his grenade throwing, had made two mistakes: He had kept his finger on the trigger of his weapon, and the safety was off.

Petraeus, observing from 40 yards away, grunted and stepped back, but didn't fall. Keane, standing next to Petraeus, looked over. "Dave, you're shot," he said. The bullet from the soldier's weapon had pierced Petraeus in the right side of his chest, just above the A in PETRAEUS on his fatigues, and clipped both a lung and an artery.

During 1993–94, Petraeus continued his long association with the 101st Airborne Division (Air Assault) as the division's Assistant Chief of Staff, G-3 (plans, operations and training) and installation Director of Plans, Training, and Mobilization (DPTM).

In 1995, he was assigned to the United Nations Mission in Haiti Military Staff as its Chief Operations Officer during Operation Uphold Democracy.

Operation Uphold Democracy

Operation Uphold Democracy (19 September 1994 – 31 March 1995) was an intervention designed to remove the military regime installed by the 1991 Haitian coup d'état that overthrew the elected President Jean-Bertrand Aristide. The operation was effectively authorized by the 31 July 1994 United Nations Security Council Resolution 940.

Aristide meeting U.S. President Bill Clinton in the White House in 1994

The operation began with the alert of United States and its allies for a forced entry into the island nation of Haiti. U.S. Navy and Air Force elements staged to Puerto Rico and southern Florida to prepare to support the airborne invasion, spearheaded by elements of 3rd Special Forces Group (Airborne) and the 10th Mountain Division. These elements were staged out of Guantanamo Bay, Cuba. The operation was directed by Commander, Joint Task Force 120 (JTF-120), provided by Commander, Carrier Group Two.

As these forces prepared to invade, including elements of the 82nd Airborne already in the air, a diplomatic element led by former President Jimmy Carter, U.S. Senator Sam Nunn and retired Chairman of the Joint Chiefs of Staff General Colin Powell persuaded the leaders of Haiti to step down and allow the elected officials to return to power.

Colin Powell

This effort was successful due in part because the U.S. delegation was able to point to the massed forces poised to enter the country. The military mission changed from a combat operation to a peace-keeping and nation-building operation at that point with the deployment of the U.S. led multinational force in Haiti.

This force was made up primarily of members of the 3rd Special Forces Group, but also included members of the 101st Military Police Company (Ft. Campbell, KY), and Marine Forces Caribbean. Teams were deployed throughout the country to establish order and humanitarian services. Regular Army forces consisting of units from the 10th Mountain Division occupied Port-au-Prince and elements from the Army Materiel Command provided logistical support in the form of the Joint Logistics Support Command (JLSC) which provided oversight and direct control over all Multinational Force and US deployed logistics units. This included the 46th Support Group, the Joint Material Management Center, JMMC and the follow on civilian contractor LOGCAP. The U.S. Coast Guard played a significant role in the operation, providing command, control and communications services from 378' cutters anchored in Port-au-Prince Harbor. The 10th Mountain Division was relieved in place by units of the 25th Infantry Division (Light) under command of Major General George Fisher.

The 25th Infantry Division deployed on 4 January 1995 from their home station of Schofield Barracks, Hawaii and officially assumed command authority from the 10th Division on 9 January 1995. General Fisher and the 25th Infantry Division were the headquarters element of what is officially known as the Multinational Forces, Combined Task Force 190, and Republic of Haiti.

The US Army Reserve unit, 458th Transportation Detachment (ATMCT), Belleville, Illinois, was activated and reported to Fort Bragg, North Carolina within 48 hours of notification.

This was the fastest a Reserve unit has ever been deployed. The 458th manned the 18th Corps Joint Movement Control Center (JMCC) in support of the mission.

Operation Uphold Democracy officially ended on 31 March 1995 when it was replaced by the UN Mission in Haiti (UNMIH). U.S. President Bill Clinton and Haitian President Jean Bertrand Aristide presided over the change of authority ceremony.

From the March 1995 until March 1996, 2,400 US personnel from the original Operation Uphold Democracy remained as a support group commanded by UNMIH under a new operation called Operation New Horizons. A large contingent of U.S. troops (USFORHAITI) participated as peacekeepers in the UNMIH until 1996 (and the U.S. forces commander was also the commander of the UN forces). UN forces under various mission names were in Haiti from 1995 through 2000. During the operation, one U.S. service member was killed by hostile fire. He was a US Special Forces Staff Sergeant shot during a roadside check.

Three Argentine Navy corvettes of the Drummond class joined the mission to force the commercial embargo of Haiti.

Operation New Horizons

Is a series of recurring U.S.-led operations in Central and South America and the Caribbean Islands. It has had several names over the years, including New Horizons and Beyond the Horizons (as of 2008). U.S. Southern Command sponsors these operations and uses active duty, reserve and National Guard forces from throughout the United States to conduct the missions. The units involved focus on engineering type endeavors to enhance the infrastructure of a region by building schools, medical clinics and roads and similar projects. The units also conduct medical assistance by providing such support to an area. Joint Task Force Bravo coordinates a number of these activities. In addition, these operations often include non-military assistance, such as from the United States Agency for International Development and the United States Department of Agriculture.

His next command, from 1995–97, was the 1st Brigade, 82nd Airborne Division, centered on the 504th Parachute Infantry Regiment. At that post, his brigade's training cycle at Fort Polk's Joint Readiness Training Center for low-intensity warfare was chronicled by novelist and military enthusiast Tom Clancy in his book *Airborne*.

From 1997–99 Petraeus served in the Pentagon as Executive Assistant to the Director of the Joint Staff and then to the Chairman of the Joint Chiefs, Gen. Henry Shelton, who described Petraeus as "a high-energy individual who likes to lead from the front, in any field he is going into".

Operation Desert Spring

In 1999, as a brigadier general, Petraeus returned to the 82nd, serving as the assistant division commander for operations and then, briefly, as acting commanding general. During his time with the 82nd, he deployed to Kuwait as part of Operation Desert Spring, the continuous rotation of combat forces through Kuwait during the decade after the Gulf War.

Operation Desert Spring was part of an ongoing operation in Kuwait by the United States that was established on December 31, 1998, following Operation Desert Storm and Operation Desert Shield. The mission objective is to maintain a forward presence and provide control and force protection over the military of Kuwait.

Operation Desert Spring ended with the beginning of Operation Iraqi Freedom on 18 March 2003.

Participants in Operation Desert Spring are entitled to receive the Armed Forces Expeditionary Medal.

Armed Forces Expeditionary Medal

2000s

From the 82nd, he moved on to serve as Chief of Staff of XVIII Airborne Corps at Fort Bragg during 2000–2001. In 2000, Petraeus suffered his second major injury, when, during a civilian skydiving jump, his parachute collapsed at low altitude due to a hook turn, resulting in a hard landing that broke his pelvis.

He was selected for promotion to Major General in 2001. During 2001–2002, as a brigadier general, Petraeus served a ten-month tour in Bosnia and Herzegovina as part of Operation Joint Forge. In Bosnia, he was the NATO Stabilization Force Assistant Chief of Staff for Operations as well as the Deputy Commander of the U.S. Joint Interagency Counter-Terrorism Task Force, a command created after the September 11 attacks to add counterterrorism capability to the U.S. forces attached to the NATO command in Bosnia.

In 2004, he was promoted to Lieutenant General. In 2007, he was promoted to General. On April 23, 2008, Secretary of Defense Gates announced that President Bush was nominating General Petraeus to command U.S. Central Command (USCENTCOM), headquartered in Tampa, Florida. The nomination required and received Senate confirmation. He was confirmed by the Senate on June 30, 2010, and took over command from temporary commander Lieutenant-General Sir Nick Parker on July 4, 2010.

Official Portrait of Secretary of Defense Robert Gates

NATO Parliamentary Assembly's Defence and Security Committee

The delegation engaged in an extensive discussion about the Alliance's future with NATO's Supreme Allied Commander Transformation General Stéphane Abrial. Challenges in the Afghanistan/Pakistan region and the broader Middle East were the principal subjects of the delegation's meeting with General David Petraeus, Combatant Commander of Central Command, as well as with Admiral Eric Olson, Commander of Special Operations Command.

Involvement in the Iraq War

101st Airborne Division

History and background of the 101st Airborne Division (Air Assault)

"Screaming Eagle"

The 101st Airborne Division (Air Assault) at Fort Campbell, Kentucky, began a transformation effort on 16 September 2004 to the US Army's new modular force structure. The major elements of the transformation included the reorganization of support elements and their command relationships, and the addition of a fourth Brigade Combat Team. As of June 2006, the division had reorganized into four Brigade Combat Teams (Unit of Action)s, two Aviation BCTs (UA)s and a support UA. Also added was a Special Troops Battalion (501st Special Troops Battalion) at Division level (in addition to similar formations in each of the Division's brigades). The Division Support Command (DISCOM), Division Artillery (DIVARTY), and 101st Corps Support Group were all stood down, with the Division Support Command being reactivated as the 101st Sustainment Brigade (incorporating a number of elements of the 101st CSG). Other elements were formed into Brigade Support Battalions. Elements of the 101st DIVARTY were deactivated and reactivated to the Division's 4 Brigade Combat Teams. Elements of the 101st Military Police Company, 311th Military Intelligence Battalion, and 501st Signal Battalion were integrated into Brigade Special Troops Battalions, and these units were inactivated.

The 101st Airborne Division (Air Assault) at Fort Campbell, Kentucky, has a mission to provide forcible entry capability through heliborne 'air assault' operations. Capable of inserting a 4,000 soldier combined arms task force, 150-kilometers into enemy terrain in one lift, and possessing 281 helicopters, including three battalions of Apache attack helicopters, the division was one of the most versatile in the Army. For this reason, the 101st Airborne Division (Air Assault) was said to be the division most in demand by combatant commanders.

The 101st stood as the Army's and world's only air assault division with unequaled strategic and tactical mobility. The 101st was unique in that it normally conducted operations 150 to 300 kilometers beyond the line of contact or forward-line-of-own-troops, requiring theater- and national-level intelligence support as a matter of course.

The 101st Airborne Division (Air Assault) demonstrated the characteristics of military professionalism since the unit's activation. On 19 August 1942, the first commander, Maj. Gen. William C. Lee, promised his new recruits that the 101st had no history, but it had a "Rendezvous with destiny." As a division, the 101st never failed that prophecy. During World War II, the 101st Airborne Division led the way on D-Day in the night drop prior to the invasion. When surrounded at Bastogne, Brig. Gen. Anthony McAuliffe answered "NUTS!" and the Screaming Eagles fought on until the siege was lifted. For their valiant efforts and heroic deeds during World War II, the 101st Airborne Division was awarded four campaign streamers and two Presidential Unit Citations.

General Order Number Five, which gave birth to the division, reads, "The 101st Airborne Division, activated at Camp Claiborne, Louisiana, has no history, but it has a rendezvous with destiny. Like the early American pioneers whose invincible courage was the foundation stone of this nation, we have broken with the past and its traditions in order to establish our claim to the future. Due to the nature of our armament, and the tactics in which we shall perfect ourselves, we shall be called upon to carry out operations of far-reaching military importance and we shall habitually go into action when the need is immediate and extreme. Let me call you attention to the fact that our badge is the great American eagle. This is a fitting emblem for a division that will crush its enemies by falling upon them like a thunderbolt from the skies. The history we shall make, the record of high achievement we hope to write in the annals of the American Army and the American people, depends wholly and completely on the men of this division. Each individual, each officer and each enlisted man, must therefore regard himself as a necessary part of a complex and powerful instrument for the overcoming of the enemies of the nation. Each, in his own job, must realize that he is not only a means, but an indispensable means for obtaining the goal of victory. It is, therefore, not too much to say that the future itself, in whose molding we expect to have our share, is in the hands of the soldiers of the 101st Airborne Division."

After the 101st was formed, only the toughest men were allowed to serve. The Division needed men that could survive being dropped from an airplane behind enemy lines and still fight and win. Only 1 in 3 men passed the selection criteria to serve in the 101st which included a 140 mile foot march in 3 days and rigorous airborne training. In September of 1943 after the Division had completed its Airborne training, it moved to England to prepare for war.

On June 5th, 1944 the Division prepared for its first combat operation, the airborne invasion of Normandy. The 101st would drop 6,700 soldiers behind enemy lines to disrupt the Germans before the massive allied beach assault on the coast of Normandy. As soon as the planes caring the soldiers of the 101st flew into France, they began receiving heavy antiaircraft fire from the Germans. The pilots took evasive action and broke formation to avoid being hit. As a result, soldiers jumped at an altitude of 300 feet at a speed of 200 mph instead of the planned 700 feet at 100 mph. This caused the Division to be scattered all over Normandy. Soldiers landed far from their units, behind enemy lines, and alone. Many were killed before they hit the ground by Germans firing into the sky.

By the end of the 1st day of the Normandy invasion, only 1 in 3 soldiers had found their unit. The scattered jump into Normandy confused the Germans just as much as it confused the Americans. The Germans did not know where to fight the Americans for there were no real front lines. Fighting consisted of small unit actions.

During the 2nd day of the invasion the 101st began to regroup and receive resupplies by gliders, many of which crashed on landing. During the next 2 days of fighting the 101st took objectives behind Utah beach and turned south towards Carentan, which was key to controlling the peninsula. The Germans had been ordered to fight to the last man. After days of heavy fighting, the 101st took Carentan. The division held the town for 2 more days under a heavy German counter attack until reinforcements arrived.

One month after jumping into Europe, the 101st mission in Normandy was complete, 1 in 4 men had been killed or wounded.

In September, 1944 the 101st jumped into Holland to conduct Operation Market Garden. The mission was to jump behind enemy lines to seize the highway running north to the Rhine river so allied tanks could advance into Germany. This highway was known as "hell's highway," and paved the way for the allied advance. 600 gliders landed in Holland, bringing in half the division. This jump was much more organized than the previous jump into Normandy. The 101st mission was to secure the southern end of the highway. It completed this mission in 2 days. The division was responsible for 60 miles of road and 16 miles of highway. 101st was next sent to the front lines near Arnhem.

On December 17th, 1944 over 12,000 101st soldiers were sent south to fight in what would be known as the Battle of the Bulge. The 101st arrived in Bastonge just ahead of the Germans and took control of the city. The Division formed a perimeter around Bastonge and held the city against fierce German fire. The Germans surrounded the town and cut off all roads. The division was cut off without supplies and was a sitting target for German artillery. The division had been deployed to Bastonge so quickly many soldiers had to endure the harsh winter without winter clothes.

After 5 days of withstanding attacks by the Germans without reinforcements or supplies, two German Officers were sent to the American Headquarters with a letter from the German Commander demanding that the 101st surrender. After hearing that the Germans wanted the 101st to surrender, the Acting Commander BG General McAuliffe said "Nuts." Surrendering was not an option for the 101st so "Nuts" was chosen as the official response to the Germans demand for surrender. The Germans continued their attack of the American perimeter without success, and the 101st continued to hold the city.

On 26 December 1944, the 101st was relieved by General Patton's 3rd Army and the siege of Bastonge ended. The 101st continued to fight, pushing the Germans back towards their own border and eventually into Germany itself. The Division entered the town of Burtchesgartens where Hitler's fortified residence "The Eagles Nest" was located. The soldiers walked through Hitler's personal residence and enjoyed the comforts of his personal retreat.

The 101st Airborne Division was reactivated as a training unit at Camp Breckinridge, Kentucky in 1948 and again in 1950, after having been inactivated following the Second World War. It was reactivated again in 1954 at Fort Jackson, South Carolina. In May 1954, the 101st reappeared as a training unit at Ft, Jackson, South Carolina, and in 1956 was transferred, less personnel and equipment to Ft. Campbell, Kentucky, for reorganization as a combat division. Official reactivation ceremonies were held on 21 September 1956. Subsequent activities included major training exercises, duty in civil disturbances and maintenance of full readiness as part of the Strategic Army Corps (STRAC).

In 1965 the Division was deployed to Vietnam. The 1st Brigade and support troops were deployed to the Republic of Vietnam, followed by the rest of the division in late 1967. In almost seven years of combat in Vietnam, elements of the 101st participated in as many as 15 campaigns.

In 1968, the 101st took on the structure and equipment of an Airmobile Division. The 101st was now using helicopters to transport troops and supplies. This new advantage made the 101st an obvious choice for the Vietnam Conflict. Dense jungle made the use of helicopters highly desirable because of the maneuverability helicopters offer. This ability allowed the 101st to accomplish more missions than any other unit.

The 101st fought in both the Tet Offensive and the Tet Counter Offensive. As part of the Tet Counter Offensive the 101st took part in the offensive operation against entrenched North Vietnamese troops on Hill 932. This hill came to be known as "Hamburger Hill." So much fire power was used that the hill was stripped of vegetation. This was still not enough to remove the entrenched North Vietnamese soldiers. Soldiers from the 101st repeatedly attacked these positions, often under heavy machine gun fire. The North Vietnamese withdrew from their positions after 10 days of fighting, and the Americans took the hill.

The 101st was the last combat division to leave Vietnam. The Screaming Eagles left Vietnam in 1972. The 101st suffered twice as many casualties in Vietnam as it did in World War II, but further established a reputation as an excellent fighting force. Seventeen 101st soldiers were awarded the Medal of Honor.

In February 1974, Major General Sidney B. Berry, Commanding General, signed Division General Order 179, authorizing wear of the Airmobile Badge. Later this was redesignated the Air

Assault Badge and approved for Army wide wear in January 1978. Finally, on 4 October 1974, the 101st Airborne Division (Air Mobile) became the 101st Airborne Division (Air Assault).

In March 1982, elements of the 101st began a six month peace keeping tour of duty in the Sinai as part of the Multinational Force and Observers. Tragedy struck in December 1985, when 248 Screaming Eagles died in a plane crash returning from the Middle East.

In August, 1990 the Iraqi Army invaded Kuwait. The US responded by deploying troops to Saudi Arabia with one the first units to deploy being the 101st. The division fired the first shots of Operation Desert Storm by taking out Iraqi radar sites on 17 January 1991. After the ground war began, the 101st was ordered to go deep into Iraq and set up a base of operations for further attacks. During the ground war phase of the operation, the 101st made the longest and largest Air Assault in history. More than 2,000 men, 50 transport vehicles, artillery, and tons of fuel and ammunition were airlifted 50 miles into Iraq. Units from the division Air Assaulted into Iraq and set up Forward Operation Base (FOB) Cobra. Land vehicles took another 2,000 troops into Iraqi territory west of Kuwait to allow US Armored Forces unrestricted access to Iraq. The 101st was responsible for seizing highway 8, which was used to resupply the Iraqi Army from Baghdad. The division moved from FOB Cobra to set up FOB Viper, which was used as a base of operations to attack Iraqi Army units withdrawing from the Kuwait border. A cease fire was declared within 100 hours of the US launching the ground war. Five soldiers from the 101st lost their lives during the ground war. With the cease fire established on 27 February 1991, the division began preparations for redeployment. By 1 May 1, 1991, the Screaming Eagles were home.

Fort Campbell soldiers supported humanitarian relief efforts in Rwanda and Somalia, then later supplied peacekeepers to Haiti and Bosnia.

A press release issued on 6 February 2003 by the 101st Airborne Division stated that elements of the entire Division had been ordered to deploy in support of the war on terrorism. The 101st Corps Support Group and the 86th Combat Support Hospital were also involved in the deployment. Previously elements of the 101st Airborne Division had been deployed to Afghanistan as part of Operation Enduring Freedom.

The Military Sealift Command reported on 11 February 2003 that the USNS Dahl and the USNS Bob Hope were loading military cargo, in Jacksonville, Florida, for the 101st Airborne Division, Fort Campbell, Kentucky, as part of the repositioning of US forces in support of the President's global war on terrorism. Cargo included Army Blackhawk, Apache, Kiowa and Chinook helicopters and a variety of wheeled vehicles. Together, the two had a capacity of more than 600,000 square feet of military cargo. It was thought that the ships would depart by 15 February 2003 and that it would take roughly 21 days to arrive in the CENTCOM AOR.

As of 8 AM (eastern) on 27 February 2003 there were roughly 10 civilian aircraft at Fort Campbell preparing to transport the first elements of the 101st Airborne Division from the United States to Kuwait. Elements of the 101st began to arrive in Kuwait on or about February 28th, 2003. The 101st Airborne Division took part in the preparations in Kuwait and the initial actions of Operation Iraqi Freedom.

In 2004 the 101st Airborne Division began returning home to Fort Campbell as part of the planned transition to the US Army's new modular force structure. This transition was largely completed by 2006, with converted elements of the Division redeploying to Iraq as early as 2005.

In 2008 the 101st Airborne Division became the lead element for US forces in Afghanistan assigned both to Operation Enduring Freedom - Afghanistan and the NATO-led International Security Assistance Force. The Combined Joint Task Force, previously led by the 82nd Airborne, became Combined Joint Task Force 101 (CJTF-101). Elements of the 101st Airborne Division including the 101st Airborne Division Headquarters and 101st Sustainment Brigade, along with the 4th Brigade Combat Team/506th Regimental Combat Team and 101st Aviation Brigade were subsequently deployed to the region. Other elements of the 101st Division remained deployed in Iraq in continued support of Operation Iraqi Freedom.

Operation Enduring Freedom

Soldiers of the 187th Infantry return from Operation Anaconda in March 2002

The 101st Airborne Division (Air Assault) was the first conventional unit to deploy in support of the American War on Terrorism. The 2d Brigade, "Strike", built around the 502d Infantry, was largely deployed to Kosovo on peacekeeping operations, with some elements of 3rd Battalion, 502nd, deploying after 9/11 as a security element in the U.S. CENTCOM AOR with the Fort Campbell-based 5th Special Forces Group. The Division quickly deployed its 3rd Brigade, the 187th Infantry's *Rakkasans*, as the first conventional unit to fight as part of Operation Enduring Freedom.

"Operation Enduring Freedom" (OEF)" is the official name used by the U.S. government for the War in Afghanistan, together with a number of smaller military actions, under the umbrella of the Global "War on Terror" (GWOT).

The operation was originally called "Operation Infinite Justice" (often misquoted as "Operation Ultimate Justice"), but as similar phrases have been used by adherents of several religions as an exclusive description of God, it is believed to have been changed to avoid offense to Muslims, who are the majority religion in Afghanistan. U.S. President George W. Bush's remark that "this crusade, this war on terrorism, is going to take a while", which prompted widespread criticism from the Islamic world, may also have contributed to the renaming of the operation.

George W. Bush

After an intense period of combat in rugged Shoh-I-Khot Mountains of eastern Afghanistan during Operation Anaconda with elements of the 10th Mountain Division, the *Rakkasans* redeployed to Fort Campbell only to find the 101st awaiting another deployment order. In 2008, the 101st 4th BCT Red and White "Currahee" including the 1st and the 2nd Battalions, 506th Infantry "Band of Brothers" were deployed to Afghanistan. The 101st Combat Aviation Brigade deployed to Afghanistan as Task Force Destiny in early 2008 to Bagram Air Base. 159th Combat Aviation Brigade deployed as Task Force Thunder for 12 months in early 2009, and again in early 2011.

Operation Anaconda

Operation Anaconda took place in early March 2002 in which the United States military and CIA Paramilitary Officers, working with allied Afghan military forces, and other North Atlantic Treaty Organization (NATO) and non-NATO forces attempted to destroy al-Qaeda and Taliban forces. The operation took place in the Shahi-Kot Valley and Arma Mountains southeast of Zormat. This operation was the first large-scale battle in the United States War in Afghanistan since the Battle of Tora Bora in December 2001. This was the first operation in the Afghanistan theater to involve a large number of U.S. conventional (i.e. non-Special Operations Forces) forces participating in direct combat activities.

Between March 2 and March 16, 2002 1,700 airlifted U.S. troops and 1,000 pro-government Afghan militia battled between 300 to 1,000 al-Qaeda and Taliban fighters to obtain control of the valley. The Taliban and al-Qaida forces fired mortars and heavy machine guns from entrenched positions in the caves and ridges of the mountainous terrain at U.S. forces attempting to secure the area. Afghan Taliban commander Maulavi Saifur Rehman Mansoor later led Taliban reinforcements to join the battle. U.S. forces had estimated the strength of the rebels in the Shahi-Kot Valley at 150 to 200, but later information suggested the actual strength was of 500 to 1,000 fighters. The U.S. forces estimated they had killed at least 500 fighters over the duration of the battle, however journalists later noted that only 23 bodies were found - and critics suggested that after a couple days, the operation "was more driven by media obsession, than military necessity".

March 15, 2002 Shah-i-Kot Valley

Arma Mountains

In March 2010, the 101st Combat Aviation Brigade deployed again to Afghanistan as Task Force Destiny to Kandahar Airfield to be the aviation asset in southern Afghanistan.

Operation Iraqi Freedom

3rd Battalion, 327th Infantry Regiment alongside Task Force 20 at Uday and Qusay Hussein's hideout

In 2003, Major General David H. Petraeus ("Eagle 6") led the Screaming Eagles to war during the 2003 invasion of Iraq (Operation Iraqi Freedom). General Petraeus led the division into Iraq saying, "Guidons, Guidons. This is Eagle 6. The 101st Airborne Division's next Rendezvous with Destiny is North to Baghdad. Op-Ord Desert Eagle 2 is now in effect. Godspeed. Air Assault. Out." The division was in V Corps, providing support to the 3rd Infantry Division by clearing Iraqi strongpoints which that division had bypassed. 3rd Battalion, 187th Infantry (3rd Brigade) was attached to 3rd Infantry Division and was the main effort in clearing Saddam International Airport. The division then went on to a tour of duty as part of the occupation forces of Iraq, using the city of Mosul as their primary base of operations. 1st and 2d Battalion, 327th Infantry Regiment (1st Brigade) oversaw the remote airfield Qayarrah West 30 miles (48 km) south of Mosul. The 502d Infantry Regiment (2d Brigade) and 3d Battalion, 327th Infantry Regiment were responsible for Mosul itself while the 187th Infantry Regiment (3d Brigade) controlled Tal Afar just west of Mosul.

Once replaced by the first operational Stryker Brigade, the 101st was withdrawn in early 2004 for rest and refit. As part of the Army's modular transformation, the existing infantry brigades, artillery brigade, and aviation brigades were transformed. The Army also activated the 4th Brigade Combat Team, which includes the 1st and 2nd Battalions, 506th Infantry Regiment ("Currahee") and subordinate units. Both battalions were part of the 101st in Vietnam but saw their colors inactivated during an Army-wide reflagging of combat battalions in the 1980s.

The reconfiguration of 101st formed seven major units in the division (four infantry BCTs, two combat aviation brigades (CABs), and one sustainment brigade), making it the largest formation currently in the U.S. Army.

As of December 2007, 143 members of the division have died while on service in Iraq.

Second deployment to Iraq

A silhouette photo of soldiers from Battery B, 3d Battalion, 320th Field Artillery Regiment, 101st Airborne Division, pose at the end of a patrol near Wynot, Iraq much like the cover of Band of Brothers

The division's second deployment to Iraq began in the late summer of 2005. The division headquarters replaced the 42d Infantry Division, which had been directing security operations as the headquarters for Task Force Liberty. Renamed Task Force Band of Brothers, the 101st assumed responsibility on 1 November 2005 for four provinces in north central Iraq: Salah ad Din, As Sulymaniyah. On 30 December 2005, Task Force Band of Brothers also assumed responsibility for training Iraqi security forces and conducting security operations in Ninevah and Dahuk provinces as the headquarters for Task Force Freedom was disestablished.

During the second deployment, 2d and 4th Brigades of the 101st Airborne Division were assigned to conduct security operations under the command of Task Force Baghdad, led initially by 3d Infantry Division, which was replaced by 4th Infantry Division. The 1st Battalion of the 506th Infantry (4th Brigade) was separated from the division and served with the Marines in Ramadi, in the Al Anbar province. 3d Brigade was assigned to Salah ad Din and Bayji sectors and 1st Brigade was assigned to the overall Kirkuk province which included Hawijah, one of the deadliest cities in Iraq.

Task Force Band of Brothers' primary mission during its second deployment to Iraq was the training of Iraqi security forces. When the 101st returned to Iraq, there were no Iraqi units capable of assuming the lead for operations against Iraqi and foreign terrorists. As the division concluded its tour, 33 battalions were in the lead for security in assigned areas, and two of four Iraq divisions in northern Iraq were commanding and controlling subordinate units.

Simultaneously with training Iraqi soldiers and their leaders, 101st soldiers conducted numerous security operations against terrorist cells operating in the division's assigned, six-province area of operations. Operation Swarmer was the largest air assault operation conducted in Iraq since 22 April 2003.

Operation Swarmer

Operation Swarmer was a joint U.S-Iraqi air assault offensive targeting insurgents in Salahuddin province, near the central city of Samarra, Iraq.

According to the US military, it was the largest air assault in Iraq since the U.S. invasion in 2003. The area was a hotbed for insurgent activity including the kidnapping and killing of civilians and soldiers. Samarra was the site of the bombing of the revered Al-Askari Shiite Shrine on 22 February 2006, which set off a wave of sectarian killing that claimed almost 500 lives. Coalition forces said they had captured a number of weapons caches containing shells, explosives and military uniforms. The US military expected this operation to last several days. Iraqi Foreign Minister Hoshyar Zebari stated that insurgents were "trying to create another Fallujah". The Operation netted at least 48 suspects, of which about 17 were released. The U.S Military reports no significant resistance, and also says it achieved the tactical surprise factor it was seeking.

Iraqi Foreign Minister Hoshyar Zebari

Other reports, however, have suggested that the lack of resistance may have been due to a lack of significant targets in the region. *Time* magazine's Brian Bennett reported that the area is a farming community with only 1,500 residents. *Time* also contested early television news reports that the operation was the largest use of air power since the 2003 invasion of Iraq, indicating that no air strikes had occurred. Bennett points out that the military term air assault refers specifically to moving troops into an area. Reporter Christopher Allbritton further reports that no fixed-wing aircraft were involved in the operation. However, the lack of fixed-wing aircraft and the use of airstrikes does not mean that the mission was not, by definition, an air assault.

1st Brigade conducted Operation Scorpion with Iraqi units near Kirkuk.

Operation Scorpion

Operation Scorpion was a joint U.S-Iraqi air assault offensive targeting insurgents near Kirkuk, Iraq. It was led by Iraqi command and targeted 8 villages in the area. Fifty-two suspected insurgents were detained.

Developing other aspects of Iraqi society also figured in 101st operations in Iraq. Division commander Major General Thomas Turner hosted the first governors' conference for the six provinces in the division's area of operations, as well as the neighboring province of Erbil. Numerous civil affairs operations were directed by the division, including the construction and renovation of schools, clinics, police stations, and other important landmarks in civilian communities from Turkey to Baghdad and from the Syrian border to the Iranian border.

Major General Thomas Turner

Return to Afghanistan

While the 1st, 2nd and 3rd Brigade Combat Teams were deployed to Iraq 2007–2008, the division headquarters, 4th Brigade Combat Team (506th Infantry Regiment), the 101st Sustainment Brigade, and the 101st Aviation Brigade followed by the 159th Aviation Brigade were deployed to Afghanistan for one-year tours falling within the 2007–2009 window.

2010 Deployments to Afghanistan

The Division Headquarters, 101st Combat Aviation Brigade (101st Aviation Regiment), 1st Brigade Combat Team (327th Infantry Regiment), 2nd Brigade Combat Team (502nd Infantry Regiment), 3rd Brigade Combat Team (187th Infantry Regiment), and 4th Brigade Combat Team (506th Infantry Regiment), and the 101st Sustainment Brigade deployed to Afghanistan in 2010. This is the first time since returning from Iraq in 2006 where all four infantry brigades (plus one CAB, SUSBDE) have served in the same combat theater. As of 5 June 2011, 131 soldiers had been killed during this deployment, the highest death toll to the 101st Airborne in any single deployment since the Vietnam War.

Maj. Gen. David H. Petraeus (right), commanding general, 101st Airborne Division (Air Assault), looks on as Lt. Gen. William S. Wallace, V Corps commanding general speaks to soldiers, March 21, 2003, Kuwait.

In 2003, Petraeus, then a Major General, saw combat for the first time when he commanded the 101st Airborne Division during V Corps's drive to Baghdad. In a campaign chronicled in detail by Pulitzer Prize-winning author Rick Atkinson of *The Washington Post* in the book *In the Company of Soldiers*, Petraeus led his division through fierce fighting south of Baghdad, in Karbala, Hilla and Najaf. Following the fall of Baghdad, the division conducted the longest heliborne assault on record in order to reach Ninawa Province, where it would spend much of 2003. The 1st Brigade was responsible for the area south of Mosul, the 2nd Brigade for the city itself, and the 3rd Brigade for the region stretching toward the Syrian border.

Statue of Saddam Hussein being toppled in Firdos Square

An often-repeated story of Petraeus' time with the 101st is his asking of embedded *The Washington Post* reporter Rick Atkinson to "Tell me how this ends," an anecdote he and other journalists have used to portray Petraeus as an early recognizer of the difficulties that would follow the fall of Baghdad.

In Mosul, a city of nearly two million people, Petraeus and the 101st employed classic counterinsurgency methods to build security and stability, including conducting targeted kinetic operations and using force judiciously, jump-starting the economy, building local security forces, staging elections for the city council within weeks of their arrival, overseeing a program of public works, reinvigorating the political process, and launching 4,500 reconstruction projects in Iraq. This approach can be attributed to Petraeus, who had been steeped in nation-building during his previous tours in nations such as Bosnia and Haiti and thus approached nation-building as a central military mission and who was "prepared to act while the civilian authority in Baghdad was still getting organized," according to Michael Gordon of *The New York Times*. Some Iraqis gave Petraeus the nickname 'King David', which was later adopted by some of his colleagues. In 2004, *Newsweek* stated that "It's widely accepted that no force worked harder to win Iraqi hearts and minds than the 101st Air Assault Division led by Petraeus."

Petraeus on patrol in Mosul with Gen. Peter J. Schoomaker, 2003

One of the General's major public works was the restoration and re-opening of the University of Mosul. Petraeus strongly supported the use of commanders' discretionary funds for public works, telling Coalition Provisional Authority director L. Paul Bremer "Money is ammunition" during the director's first visit to Mosul. Petraeus' often repeated catchphrase was later incorporated into official military briefings and was also eventually incorporated into the U.S. Army Counterinsurgency Field Manual drafted with Petraeus' oversight.

In February 2004, the 101st was replaced in Mosul by a portion of I Corps headquarters, but operational forces consisted solely of a unit roughly one quarter its size—a Stryker brigade. The following summer, the Governor of Nineveh Province was assassinated and most of the Sunni Arab Provincial Council members walked out in the ensuing selection of the new governor, leaving Kurdish members in charge of a predominantly Sunni Arab province. Later that year, the local police commander defected to the Kurdish Minister of Interior in Irbil after repeated assassination attempts against him, attacks on his house, and the kidnapping of his sister. The largely Sunni Arab police collapsed under insurgent attacks launched at the same time Coalition Forces attacked Fallujah in November 2004.

There are differing explanations for the apparent collapse of the police force in Mosul. *The Guardian* quoted an anonymous US diplomat saying "Mosul basically collapsed after he [Petraeus] left". Former diplomat Peter Galbraith criticized Petraeus' command of the 101st, saying his achievements have been exaggerated and his reputation is inflated. He wrote for *The New York Review of Books* that "Petraeus ignored warnings from America's Kurdish allies that he was appointing the wrong people to key positions in Mosul's local government and police."

On the other hand, in the book *Fiasco*, *The Washington Post* reporter Tom Ricks wrote that "Mosul was quiet while he (Petraeus) was there, and likely would have remained so had his successor had as many troops as he had—and as much understanding of counterinsurgency techniques." Ricks went on to say that "the population-oriented approach Petraeus took in Mosul in 2003 would be the one the entire U.S. Army in Iraq was trying to adopt in 2006." *Time* columnist Joe Klein largely agreed with Ricks, writing that the Stryker brigade that replaced the 101st "didn't do any of the local governance that Petraeus had done". Moving away from counterinsurgency principles, "they were occupiers, not builders." *The New York Times* reporter Michael Gordon and retired General Bernard Trainor echoed Ricks and Klein, including in their book *Cobra II* a quote that Petraeus "did it right and won over Mosul".

Maj. Gen. David H. Petraeus, commanding general, 101st Airborne Division (Air Assault)

Maj. Gen. David H. Petraeus Cites Highs and Lows of Iraqi Deployment

FORT CAMPBELL, Ky., March 17, 2004 - Home along with his soldiers after a one-year deployment in Iraq, the commander of the 101st Airborne Division (Air

Assault) called the division's experiences in Operation Iraqi Freedom "a roller coaster" of highs and lows.

Since the first elements of the division began leaving their sprawling post that straddles the Kentucky-Tennessee border north of Nashville in February 2003, Army Maj. Gen. David H. Petraeus said they experienced amazing high points in Iraq.

Division troops engaged and killed Saddam Hussein's two sons, Uday and Qusay, in Mosul, and also captured Asa Hawleri, third in the terrorist group Ansar al-Islam's chain of command. They played a peacekeeping role, presiding over the first elections in post-war Iraq and helping to rebuild the country.

But contrasting these high moments were some tremendous lows, Petraeus said, particularly the loss of 60 division soldiers in Iraq. "There is nothing tougher than the loss of a comrade in arms. There really is not," the general said.

Petraeus said his own personal low of the campaign came the night of Nov. 15, when 17 of his soldiers died in a collision of Black Hawk helicopters.

"The loss of 17 soldiers in one night when two helicopters collided over Mosul was just a blow beyond belief," he said. "It's like losing 17 children. It's almost beyond comprehension -- a terrible, terrible blow to the organization and the individuals in it."

Two months earlier, the division had experienced another devastating tragedy, this one alleged to have been inflicted by one of its own. Sgt. Hasan Akbar allegedly threw a grenade into three tents housing members of the 101st's 1st Brigade Combat Team, killing two officers and wounding 14 others. Akbar's trial is set to begin July 12.

Petraeus said the attack, launched just as the division was preparing to move north into Iraq, could have zapped his soldiers' resolve. Instead, thanks to the "tremendous response" by leaders within the brigade, Petraeus said it served as an inspiration.

"After every death came the question, what would that soldier have wanted us to do?" he said. "And the answer was to ensure that his death was not in vain and to drive on and accomplish the mission."

The morning after the Black Hawk tragedy in Mosul, Petraeus said, a young soldier in the headquarters provided similar inspiration. As he left his morning update session, struggling to think about anything but the loss of 17 soldiers, the soldier grabbed him and said, "Sir, that just gives us 17 more reasons to get this right," Petraeus recalled.

"I drew an awful lot of strength from that particular soldier that morning," he said.

Not all the division's highs and lows in Iraq were so profound, but they, too contributed to the day-to-day roller coaster effect of the deployment, Petraeus said.

In addition to the 101st's successes during the operation - from deploying to the theater in record time to successfully carrying out its warfighter role against a variety of enemy threats - the division's soldiers performed equally well in their peacekeeping role.

After the division blanketed Mosul with four infantry battalions to establish order, soldiers presided over Iraq's first postwar elections last May. Iraqis in Nineveh province elected a provincial council.

Meanwhile, the 101st oversaw the completion of more than 5,000 projects, building or rebuilding more than 500 schools and dozens of medical clinics, opening hundreds of kilometers of roads, reopening Internet cafes and putting an irrigation system back into operation. More than $57 million from Petraeus's commander's emergency reconstruction fund covered the costs.

The people of Mosul are so grateful for the 101st Airborne Division's part in the projects that this week they named a street in the division's honor. "It's wonderful recognition that they appreciate what our soldiers have done for them," Petraeus said.

Yet for every success, Petraeus said, he and his troops struggled with what he called the "man in the moon challenge."

"(The Iraqis) would ask us why we could overthrow Saddam in three weeks and why we could put a man on the moon but we couldn't give them a job right then, right there," he said. "Why we couldn't throw a switch and get the entire electrical infrastructure working again."

Expectations were enormous, he said. "We used to joke that the reward for one good deed in Iraq was a request for 10 more good deeds."

Petraeus said he has "cautious optimism" about the future of Iraq, citing the country's vast oil, water and sulphur reserves, the high education levels among the people, their entrepreneurial spirit and most of all, their willingness to work hard to achieve their goals.

The caution, he said, comes from the various groups and factions now jockeying for power in the new Iraq. "At the end of the day, there has to be a spirit of compromise that prevails to allow the new Iraq to serve the needs and hopes and dreams and aspirations of all Iraqis, not just one of these particular groups," the general said.

Now that the 17,000 soldiers under his command are back at Fort Campbell, Petraeus said he feels good about the role they played in helping overthrow Saddam Hussein and reestablish peace and stability in Iraq.

"It's the greatest privilege that I can possibly imagine to have served in this division and to be blessed with such a team that we have here, at every single level, from the soldier on up to the division staff," he said. "I think our soldiers should be very proud of what they've accomplished in Iraq, and I think all Americans should be very proud of what our soldiers did."

Maj. Gen. David H. Petraeus stops to pick up a young Iraqi boy when his convoy stopped in Karbala, Iraq, April 6.

101st Commander Calls Adaptability Key to Success in Iraq

FORT CAMPBELL, Ky., March 17, 2004 — One year ago today, the 101st Airborne Division (Air Assault) was at Camp New Jersey, the division's holding area in Kuwait, awaiting orders to move north and cross into Iraq at the onset of Operation Iraqi Freedom.

Today, with all members of the division's "Screaming Eagles" back here at their home post, division commander Maj. Gen. David H. Petraeus credited his soldiers' adaptability to ever-changing situations for ensuring the division's success in Iraq.

"The one overriding lesson out of all of this is that our flexible, adaptable soldiers are the key to everything our division and our Army did in Iraq," Petraeus said.

Throughout their deployment, Petraeus said, his soldiers continually adjusted to the situations that confronted them. "The truth is, no one approach or tactic fits everywhere in Iraq," he said. "Every place is unique, and the situations are all different. And in fact, there is no one unique tactic or approach that even works day in and day out in the same location."

Petraeus said that even in Mosul — the division's Iraqi base from April until last month — his soldiers constantly had to "adapt to the situation, to the enemy, to the resources that we had available."

But Petraeus said that adaptability demonstrated itself even before the division had left its home post. He credited his troops with breaking standard deployment conventions to get 5,000 vehicles, 1,500 shipping containers, 17,000 soldiers and 264 helicopters from Fort Campbell to

Kuwait — all within less than six weeks of receiving a formal deployment order. "They made a Herculean effort," he said, even physically joining in the ship loading at Fort Lauderdale, Fla., to speed up the process.

Despite intensive training to prepare the division's leaders for a rapid deployment and for the vast railhead, port and airfield improvements since Operation Desert Storm, Petraeus acknowledged the division felt "under the gun" as it prepared to get its equipment in place and possibly face combat "within a very, very short timeline."

With the division in theater and the countdown to war continuing, the pressure intensified, he said. "We had challenges in that our soldiers were still unloading equipment off ships as elements of the division were getting ready to go through the berm (into Iraq)," Petraeus said.

Once the war started, he said, his troops used innovative tactics to confront a variety of different enemies as they moved north — Republic Guard, Saddam Fedayeen paramilitary group fighters and Baath militia. Much of the fighting took place in large, urban areas including Najaf, a city of 600,000 people.

"Although we train for this at the Joint Readiness Training Center and home station, I'll tell you that nothing prepares you to clear a city of 600,000 as your first combat objective," Petraeus said.

He credits his young leaders and soldiers "at the point of decision" who "changed the tactics, techniques and procedures to deal with the threat that we found." Kiowa attack helicopter pilots, for example, flew in front of the U.S. forces, exhibiting what the general called "courage and initiative."

Similarly, Petraeus said the division's Apache pilots adapted to conduct daylight reconnaissance operations, supported by Air Force close-air support, the Army tactical missile system and Air Force jammers, intelligence-gathering systems and command and control systems. The combination, he said, "proved very, very effective in finding and then destroying heavy enemy elements that were on the flank of the 5th Corps advance."

As the division advanced to Baghdad, then Mosul, Petraeus said the 101st Airborne Division (Air Assault) troops adopted a new role as they began helping the Iraqis rebuild their country. He admits the soldiers' dual roles as warfighters and peacekeepers sometimes appeared to be at odds.

"Oftentimes we felt as if our soldiers had a rifle in one hand and a wrench in the other," Petraeus said. "We were fighting, but we were also rebuilding." He said the young soldiers who regularly patrolled Mosul and interacted with the Iraqi people successfully carried out these dual and seemingly conflicting roles.

"It's an enormous tribute to our young soldiers — the sergeants, lieutenants and captains who were out there every day, interacting with people all day, every day, and their ability to adjust to the situation as they find it," he said.

Now returned with his division to Fort Campbell, Petraeus said the lessons of Operation Iraqi Freedom validate what his former boss, retired chairman of the Joint Chiefs of Staff Gen. Henry "Hugh" Shelton, used to say: "It's people, not equipment. It's quality. Not quantity."

Quantity isn't a bad thing, Petraeus said. "What we would like to have is a huge quantity of very high-quality people with the best equipment money can buy," he said. "But at the end of the day, what is decisive is the people using the equipment — high-quality people."

"And that," he said, "is what we were blessed to have (in Iraq)."

Petraeus said he agrees wholeheartedly with Tom Brokaw, author of "The Greatest Generation," a book about World War II veterans, who called the men and women fighting the war on terror "the next greatest generation."

"I've seen our young soldiers endure tremendous hardship, overcome tremendous challenges, fight a tenacious, determined and even suicidal enemy, and demonstrate incredible innovativeness and compassion," he said. "It's just extraordinary."

Now that they're returned to their home station, as their equipment continues to arrive and before they get back into their full training cycles, Petraeus said he has one more adaptation to ask of his soldiers.

"What we need do right now is to make sure our soldiers get time with their families, and enjoy some of the blessings that this country enjoys that they have been fighting to protect for the past couple of years," he said.

Maj. Gen. David H. Petraeus, commanding general, 101st Airborne Division (Air Assault), gives a "thumbs-up" sign to a soldier while walking alongside a convoy in Iraq.

Multi-National Security Transition Command – Iraq

In June 2004, less than six months after the 101st returned to the U.S., Petraeus was promoted to lieutenant general and became the first commander of the Multi-National Security Transition Command Iraq. This newly created command had responsibility for training, equipping, and mentoring Iraq's growing army, police, and other security forces as well as developing Iraq's security institutions and building associated infrastructure, such as training bases, police stations, and border forts. During Petraeus' fifteen months at the helm of MNSTC-I, he stood up a three-star command virtually from scratch and in the midst of serious fighting in places like Fallujah, Mosul, and Najaf. By the end of his command, some 100,000 Iraqi Security Forces had been trained; Iraqi Army and Police were being employed in combat; countless reconstruction projects had been executed; and hundreds of thousands of weapons, body armor, and other equipment had been distributed in what was described as the "largest military procurement and distribution effort since World War II", at a cost of over $11 billion.

MNF-I patch worn by MNSTC-I

Multi-National Security Transition Command – Iraq (MNSTC-I) was the branch of the Multi-National Force - Iraq that is responsible for developing, organizing, training, equipping, and sustaining the Iraqi Security Ministries (Ministry of Defense (MoD) and Ministry of Interior (MoI)) and their associated Iraqi Security Forces (ISF), i.e. the military of Iraq and the Iraqi Police.

The stated mission was to assist MoI, MoD, and Counter Terrorism Service (CTS) by improving the quality of the ISF and institutional performances. Allowing ISF to increasingly assume responsibility for population protection and develop Iraqi security institutions capable of sustaining security with reduced Coalition involvement. Therefore, the MNSTC-I mission was a central part of the U.S. exit strategy.

MNSTC-I was commanded (since October 2009) by US Army Lieutenant General Michael D. Barbero and was headquartered in the International Zone in Baghdad at Phoenix Base, a former elementary school. It was previously commanded by US Army Lieutenant General Frank Helmick (July 2008 — October 2009), US Army Lieutenant General James M. Dubik (June 2007 — July 2008), Lieutenant General Martin E. Dempsey (September 2005 — June 2007) and Lieutenant General David H. Petraeus (June 2004 — September 2005).

The command was a direct outgrowth of the need to create a new Iraqi Army under the [Coalition Provisional Authority]. The original command consisted of the Coalition Military Assistance Transition Team (CMATT) under Major General Paul Eaton. Separate efforts under the State Department were designed to build a new police force through the [Civilian Police Assistance Team] and advisory missions to the Ministries of Defense and Interior. All of these missions were consolidated under MNSTC-I when then Lieutenant General Petraeus was tapped to take over the ISF mission.

It was originally organized into three training teams, listed below, but has since grown dramatically as newer missions and needs have been identified. The three former organizations were:

Coalition Military Assistance Training Team (CMATT), which organized, trained, and equipped the Iraqi Army.

JHQ-ST - Joint Headquarters Advisory Support Team, which assisted the joint headquarters of the Iraqi Army in developing a command and control system. Also, JHQ assisted in operational planning and gave strategic advice to the Iraqi government.

Civilian Police Assistance Training Team (CPATT), which organized, trained, and equipped the Iraqi Police.

MNSTC-I expanded from the three original organizations to consists of the following subordinate units organized under the Directorate of Defense Affairs (DDA) and Directorate of Interior Affairs (DOIA)

Coalition Army Advisory Training Team (CAATT) to build the Iraqi Army

Coalition Air Force Transition Team (CAFTT) to build the Iraqi Air Force

Maritime Strategic Transition Team (MaSTT) to support the Iraqi Navy, Marines and Coast Guard

Civilian Police Assistance Training Team (CPATT) building the various Iraqi police agencies

Intelligence Transition Team (ITT) to build the military and police information organizations

Iraqi National Counter-Terrorism Task Force (INCTF) to assist Iraqi special operations

Security Assistance Office (SAO) to assist in the purchase of equipment and overseas training

Joint Headquarters Assistance Team (JHQ-AT) to advise the Iraqi Joint Headquarters

Ministry of Defense Transition Team (MOD-TT) to advise the MoD staff

Ministry of Interior Transition Team (MOI-TT) to advise the MoI staff

In addition, the organization partnered with the NATO Training Mission - Iraq (NTM-I) as the commander of MNSTC-I is "dual hatted" as the NTM-I commander as well. In June 2009, the organization structure changed again with the creation of the Iraqi Training and Advisory Mission (ITAM) led by US Army Major General Richard J. Rowe, Jr, the Iraqi Security Assistance Mission (ISAM), and the Partnership Strategy Group (PSG-I). ITAM and ISAM, INCTF and PSG-I report to the Deputy Commanding General. ITAM is focused on institutional training while ISAM is focused on foreign military sales. Under the new ITAM structure:

Coalition Army Advisory Training Team (CAATT) became ITAM-Army

Coalition Air Force Transition Team (CAFTT) became ITAM-Air Force

Maritime Strategic Transition Team (MaSTT) became ITAM-Navy

Civilian Police Assistance Training Team (CPATT) became ITAM-Police

Intelligence Transition Team (ITT) became ITAM-Intel TT

Ministry of Defense Transition Team (MOD-TT) became ITAM-MOD

Ministry of Interior Transition Team (MOI-TT) became ITAM-MOI

Under the new PSG-I structure: Joint Headquarters Assistance Team (JHQ-AT) was absorbed into the PSG-I organization.

ISAM: The organizations under ISAM mirror ITAM, though it took over the duties of the Security Assistance Office (SAO).

- ISAM Army
- ISAM Navy
- ISAM Air Force
- ISAM Logistics/End Use Monitoring (LOG/EUM)
- ISAM International Military Education and Training/Out of Country Training (IMET/OCT)

MNSTC-I published a monthly magazine, *The Advisor*, with information on the training of the Iraqi Security Forces.

MNSTC-I was replaced by United States Forces - Iraq in 2010.

In September 2004, Petraeus wrote an article for *The Washington Post* in which he described the tangible progress being made in building Iraq's security forces from the ground up while also noting the many challenges associated with doing so. "Although there have been reverses – not to mention horrific terrorist attacks," Petraeus wrote, "there has been progress in the effort to enable Iraqis to shoulder more of the load for their own security, something they are keen to do." Some of the challenges involved in building security forces had to do with accomplishing this task in the midst of a tough insurgency—or, as Petraeus wrote, "making the mission akin to repairing an aircraft while in flight – and while being shot at". Other challenges included allegations of corruption as well as efforts to improve Iraq's supply accountability procedures. For example, according to former Interim Iraq Governing Council member Ali A. Allawi in *The Occupation of Iraq: Winning the War, Losing the Peace*, "under the very noses of the security transition command, officials both inside and outside the ministry of defense were planning to embezzle most, if not all, of the procurement budget of the army".

Here is the article that David Petraeus wrote in the Washington Post on Sunday, September 26, 2004

Battling for Iraq

By David H. Petraeus
Sunday, September 26, 2004; Page B07

BAGHDAD -- Helping organize, train and equip nearly a quarter-million of Iraq's security forces is a daunting task. Doing so in the middle of a tough insurgency increases the challenge enormously, making the mission akin to repairing an aircraft while in flight -- and while being shot at. Now, however, 18 months after entering Iraq, I see tangible progress. Iraqi security elements are being rebuilt from the ground up.

The institutions that oversee them are being reestablished from the top down. And Iraqi leaders are stepping forward, leading their country and their security forces courageously in the face of an enemy that has shown a willingness to do anything to disrupt the establishment of the new Iraq.

In recent months, I have observed thousands of Iraqis in training and then watched as they have conducted numerous operations. Although there have been reverses -- not to mention horrific terrorist attacks -- there has been progress in the effort to enable Iraqis to shoulder more of the load for their own security, something they are keen to do. The future undoubtedly will be full of difficulties, especially in places such as Fallujah. We must expect setbacks and recognize that not every soldier or policeman we help train will be equal to the challenges ahead.

Nonetheless, there are reasons for optimism. Today approximately 164,000 Iraqi police and soldiers (of which about 100,000 are trained and equipped) and an additional 74,000 facility protection forces are performing a wide variety of security missions. Equipment is being delivered. Training is on track and increasing in capacity. Infrastructure is being repaired. Command and control structures and institutions are being reestablished.

Most important, Iraqi security forces are in the fight -- so much so that they are suffering substantial casualties as they take on more and more of the burdens to achieve security in their country. Since Jan. 1 more than 700 Iraqi security force members have been killed, and hundreds of Iraqis seeking to volunteer for the police and military have been killed as well.

Six battalions of the Iraqi regular army and the Iraqi Intervention Force are now conducting operations. Two of these battalions, along with the Iraqi commando battalion, the counterterrorist force, two Iraqi National Guard battalions and thousands of policemen recently contributed to successful operations in Najaf. Their readiness to enter and clear the Imam Ali shrine was undoubtedly a key factor in enabling Grand Ayatollah Ali Sistani to persuade members of the Mahdi militia to lay down their arms and leave the shrine.

In another highly successful operation several days ago, the Iraqi counterterrorist force conducted early-morning raids in Najaf that resulted in the capture of several senior lieutenants and 40 other members of that militia, and the seizure of enough weapons to fill nearly four 7 1/2-ton dump trucks.

Within the next 60 days, six more regular army and six additional Intervention Force battalions will become operational. Nine more regular army battalions will complete training in January, in time to help with security missions during the Iraqi elections at the end of that month.

Iraqi National Guard battalions have also been active in recent months. Some 40 of the 45 existing battalions -- generally all except those in the Fallujah-Ramadi area -- are conducting operations on a daily basis, most alongside coalition forces, but many independently. Progress has also been made in police training. In the past week alone, some 1,100 graduated from the basic policing course and five specialty courses. By early spring, nine academies in Iraq and one in Jordan will be graduating a total of 5,000 police each month from the eight-week course, which stresses patrolling and investigative skills, substantive and procedural legal knowledge, and proper use of force and weaponry, as well as pride in the profession and adherence to the police code of conduct.

Iraq's borders are long, stretching more than 2,200 miles. Reducing the flow of extremists and their resources across the borders is critical to success in the counterinsurgency. As a result, with support from the Department of Homeland Security, specialized training for Iraq's border enforcement elements began earlier this month in Jordan.

Regional academies in Iraq have begun training as well, and more will come online soon. In the months ahead, the 16,000-strong border force will expand to 24,000 and then 32,000. In addition, these forces will be provided with modern technology, including vehicle X-ray machines, explosive-detection devices and ground sensors.

Outfitting hundreds of thousands of new Iraqi security forces is difficult and complex, and many of the units are not yet fully equipped. But equipment has begun flowing. Since July 1, for example, more than 39,000 weapons and 22 million rounds of ammunition have been delivered to Iraqi forces, in addition to 42,000 sets of body armor, 4,400 vehicles, 16,000 radios and more than 235,000 uniforms.

Considerable progress is also being made in the reconstruction and refurbishing of infrastructure for Iraq's security forces. Some $1 billion in construction to support this effort has been completed or is underway, and five Iraqi bases are already occupied by entire infantry brigades.

Numbers alone cannot convey the full story. The human dimension of this effort is crucial. The enemies of Iraq recognize how much is at stake as Iraq reestablishes its security forces. Insurgents and foreign fighters continue to mount barbaric attacks against police stations, recruiting centers and military installations, even though the vast majority of the population deplores such attacks. Yet despite the sensational attacks, there is no shortage of qualified recruits volunteering to join Iraqi security forces. In the past couple of months, more than 7,500 Iraqi men have signed up for the army and are preparing to report for basic training to fill out the final nine battalions of the Iraqi regular army. Some 3,500 new police recruits just reported for training in various locations. And two days after the recent bombing on a street outside a police recruiting location in Baghdad, hundreds of Iraqis were once again lined up inside the force protection walls at another location -- where they were greeted by interim Prime Minister Ayad Allawi.

I meet with Iraqi security force leaders every day. Though some have given in to acts of intimidation, many are displaying courage and resilience in the face of repeated threats and attacks on them, their families and their comrades. I have seen their determination and their desire to assume the full burden of security tasks for Iraq.

There will be more tough times, frustration and disappointment along the way. It is likely that insurgent attacks will escalate as Iraq's elections approach. Iraq's security forces are, however, developing steadily and they are in the fight. Momentum has gathered in recent months. With strong Iraqi leaders out front and with continued coalition -- and now NATO -- support, this trend will continue. It will not be easy, but few worthwhile things are.

(An Iraqi National Guard Soldier/Aladin Abdel Naby -- Reuters)

The writer, an Army lieutenant general, commands the Multinational Security Transition Command in Iraq. He previously commanded the 101st Airborne Division, which was deployed in Iraq from March 2003 until February 2004.

The Washington Post stated in August 2007 that the Pentagon had lost track of approximately 30% of weapons supplied to the Iraqi security forces. The General Accounting Office said that the weapons distribution was haphazard, rushed, and did not follow established procedures—particularly from 2004 to 2005, when security training was led by Petraeus and Iraq's security forces began to see combat in places like Najaf and Samarra.

Over a hundred thousand AK-47 assault rifles and pistols were delivered to Iraqi forces without full documentation, and some of the missing weapons may have been abducted by Iraqi insurgents. Thousands of body armor pieces have also been lost. *The Independent* has stated that the military believed "the situation on the ground was so urgent, and the agency responsible for recording the transfers of arms so short staffed, that field commanders had little choice in the matter." The Pentagon conducted its own investigation, and accountability was subsequently regained for many of the weapons.

Following his second tour in Iraq, Petraeus authored a widely read article in *Military Review*, listing fourteen observations he had made during two tours in Iraq, including: do not do too much with your own hands, money is ammunition, increasing the number of stakeholders is critical to success, success in a counterinsurgency requires more than just military operations, ultimate success depends on local leaders, there is no substitute for flexible and adaptable leaders, and, finally, a leader's most important task is to set the right tone.

Multi-National Force – Iraq (spring 2007)

Petraeus walking through Market, March 2007

In January 2007, as part of his overhauled Iraq strategy, President George W. Bush announced that Petraeus would succeed Gen. George Casey as commanding general of MNF-I to lead all U.S. troops in Iraq.

Gen. George Casey

On January 23, the Senate Armed Services Committee held Petraeus' nomination hearing, during which he testified on his ideas for Iraq, particularly the strategy underpinning the "surge" of forces. During his opening statement, Petraeus stated that "security of the population, especially in Baghdad, and in partnership with the Iraqi Security Forces, will be the focus of the military effort." He went on to state that security will require establishing a persistent presence, especially in Iraq's most threatened neighborhoods. He also noted the critical importance of helping Iraq increase its governmental capacity, develop employment programs, and improve daily life for its citizens.

Throughout Petraeus' tenure in Iraq, Multi-National Force-Iraq endeavored to work with the Government of Iraq to carry out this strategy that focuses on securing the population. Doing so required establishing—and maintaining—persistent presence by living among the population, separating reconcilable Iraqis from irreconcilable enemies, relentlessly pursuing the enemy, taking back sanctuaries and then holding areas that have been cleared, and continuing to develop Iraq's security forces and to support local security forces, often called Sons of Iraq, and to integrate them into the Iraqi Army and Police and other employment programs.

The strategy underpinning the "surge" of forces, as well as the ideas Petraeus included in US army Field Manual 3–24, *Counterinsurgency*, have been referred to by some journalists and politicians as the "Petraeus Doctrine," although the surge itself was proposed a few months before Petraeus took command. Despite the misgivings of most Democratic and a few Republican senators over the proposed implementation of the "Petraeus Doctrine" in Iraq, specifically regarding the troop surge, Petraeus was unanimously confirmed as a four-star general and MNF-I commander on January 27.

Before leaving for Iraq, Petraeus recruited a number of highly educated military officers, nicknamed "Petraeus guys" or "designated thinkers", to advise him as commander, including Col. Mike Meese, head of the Social Sciences Department at West Point and Col. H.R. McMaster, famous for his leadership at the Battle of 73 Easting in the Gulf War and in the pacification of Tal Afar more recently, as well as for his doctoral dissertation on Vietnam-era civil-military relations entitled *Dereliction of Duty*. While most of Petraeus' closest advisers are American military officers, he also hired Lt. Col. David Kilcullen of the Australian Army, who was working for the US State Department. Kilcullen upon his return from Iraq published *The Accidental Guerrilla*, and has discussed the central front of the war and lessons learned in Iraq in *The Washington Post*.

Lt. Col. David Kilcullen

New commander tough, driven

General tagged by some as man who may fix Iraq

Newspaper report Jan. 2007

Lt. Gen. David Petraeus is Bush's pick to be the top U.S. commander in Iraq.

Lt. Gen. David Petraeus, who is President Bush's choice to become the top U.S. military commander in Iraq, posed a riddle during the initial march to Baghdad four years ago that now becomes his own conundrum to solve: "Tell me how this ends."

WASHINGTON — Lt. Gen. David Petraeus, who is President Bush's choice to become the top U.S. military commander in Iraq, posed a riddle during the initial march to Baghdad four years ago that now becomes his own conundrum to solve: "Tell me how this ends."

That query, uttered repeatedly to a reporter then embedded in Petraeus's 101st Airborne Division, revealed a flinty skepticism about prospects in Iraq — by the man now asked to forestall a military debacle.

Long recognized as one of the Army's premier intellectuals, with a PhD from Princeton to complement his West Point education, Petraeus, 54, will inherit one of the toughest assignments handed any senior officer since the Vietnam War. He takes command of 132,000 U.S. troops in a country shattered by insurgency and sectarian bloodletting, with a home front that is divided and disheartened after 3,000 American combat deaths. If his riddle of 2003 remains apt, so does the headline on a Newsweek cover story about Petraeus in July 2004: "Can This Man Save Iraq?"

Skepticism is rife, inside and outside the Army. "Petraeus is being given a losing hand. I say that reluctantly. The war is unmistakably going in the wrong direction," retired Army Gen. Barry McCaffrey said in an interview. "The only good news in all this is that Petraeus is so incredibly intelligent and creative ... I'm sure he'll say to himself, 'I'm not going to be the last soldier off the roof of the embassy in the Green Zone.'"

Petraeus, if controversial among some peers who deem him arrogant or excessively ambitious, is seen by many others as perhaps the last, best hope for success in Iraq. "If anyone can pick up the baton and run with it, it is David Petraeus," said retired Gen. Gordon Sullivan, a former Army chief of staff.

After spending 2 1/2 of the past four years in Iraq, as a division commander and then as the officer overseeing the initial reconstruction of Iraqi security forces, Petraeus is known to believe that a stable, pacified Iraq is still possible — if not probable — but not without dramatically improved security. Having also served in Bosnia after the catastrophic civil war there, he has told friends that he sees troubling parallels between that country and Iraq. Two months ago, he said, "I actually stay awake occasionally at night trying to figure out the path ahead."

Upon Senate confirmation and the receipt of his fourth star, making him a full general, he is expected to spend some weeks assessing conditions in Iraq and drafting a strategic plan that goes beyond the current debate over whether to increase U.S. troop levels by up to five brigades, roughly 20,000 troops. That "surge" is consistent with the military's new counterinsurgency manual, much of which Petraeus wrote, which stresses protecting the indigenous population and imposing security as a condition for stability.

One of Petraeus's long-time Army patrons, now-retired Gen. Jack Keane, has advocated an even larger deployment this spring. But many strategists say such an increase is pointless without a sweeping economic reconstruction program and a robust rearming of the Iraqi army with artillery, attack helicopters and other heavy weapons.

Many also say the additional forces to be used in any troop increase are already badly worn down by the military's intense operational tempo since the first deployments to Afghanistan in 2001. The new Democratic leadership in Congress on Friday pointedly rejected even a short-term escalation in U.S. forces in Iraq.

These problems and more confront Petraeus, who has told friends that he has no illusions about the complexity of the job at hand. Unaccustomed to failure, he is, in the words of one former aide, "the most competitive man on the planet." The son of a Dutch sea captain who took refuge in New York during World War II, Petraeus grew up in Cornwall-on-Hudson, a few miles outside the gates of the U.S. Military Academy, which he entered as a new cadet in July 1970.

"A striver to the max, Dave was always 'going for it' in sports, academics, leadership, and even his social life," the West Point yearbook noted in 1974. A month after graduation, he married Holly Knowlton, the daughter of the academy superintendent. They have two grown children.

As a young lieutenant, Petraeus entered an Army battered by defeat in Vietnam and badly frayed by drugs, lack of discipline and the American public's diminished esteem for the military. Accolades and achievements followed as he moved from post to post. Petraeus received all three prizes awarded in his class at Ranger School, perhaps the Army's toughest physical and psychological challenge, and he later won the George C. Marshall award as the top graduate in the Army Command and General Staff College class of 1983.

As he rose through the ranks, Petraeus alternated command and staff assignments with duty as an aide to several of the Army's most prominent four-star generals, a pattern that caused one envious peer to call him a "professional son." At Princeton University, Petraeus's dissertation, "The American Military and the Lessons of Vietnam," examined the caution that seized the high command after the war.

His intensity, serrated intellect and competitiveness have rubbed some officers the wrong way. Muttered jibes about "King David" have been heard around his command post. He remains obsessive about what he calls "the P.T. culture" — physical training — and has been known to challenge soldiers half his age to various athletic competitions. "If anyone beats him in the shorter runs, four miles or so, he takes them out for ten miles and smokes them," a staff officer observed several years ago. At 5-foot-9 and 155 pounds, Petraeus evokes George Bernard Shaw's description of the British general Bernard Montgomery: "an intensely compacted hank of wire."

Twice, accidents almost ended his career, or even his life. In 1991, as a battalion commander at Fort Campbell, Ky., he was shot in the chest with an M-16 rifle when a soldier tripped during a training exercise. Rushed into surgery at Vanderbilt University Medical Center in Nashville, he underwent five hours of surgery by Bill Frist, who a decade later became Senate majority leader. While skydiving in 2000, Petraeus survived the abrupt collapse of his parachute 60 feet up. His shattered pelvis was reassembled with a plate and long screws.

As commander of the 101st Airborne, Petraeus saw combat for the first time during the division's drive up the Euphrates Valley, with sharp firefights in Najaf, Karbala and Hilla. But it was during the division's subsequent occupation of Mosul and northern Iraq that he won widespread acclaim by resurrecting the local economy, restoring services and preserving order with strategic force, which included killing Saddam Hussein's two sons. Posters in the division bivouacs read: "What have you done to win Iraqi hearts and minds today?"

More than 60 soldiers from the 101st died during the deployment, and upon bringing the division back to Kentucky in February 2004, Petraeus remarked, "It's been a long, tough year, and I am older in more ways than just age."

His subsequent service as commander of the Multi-National Security Transition Command, responsible for training Iraqi security forces, was another long, tough year that stretched to 15 months. Tens of thousands of Iraqi soldiers and police were trained, with concomitant efforts to supply infrastructure, equipment and procedures. But the project at best remains an imperiled work in progress, with alarming signs of sectarian fractures spreading through the Iraqi security institutions that Petraeus is known to consider as crucial to restoring stability there as any additional coalition forces could be.

Both long stints in Iraq have given Petraeus an intimate knowledge of the country's ethnic fractures and the limits of American influence. "A certain degree of intellectual humility is a good thing," he once told a reporter. "There aren't always a hell of a lot of absolutely right answers out there."

His cordial relations with the media, and the Newsweek cover story that depicted him as a potential savior for the Bush administration, rankled some of his superiors in the Pentagon, according to two now-retired senior generals. When Petraeus was sent to command the U.S. Army Combined Arms Center at Ft. Leavenworth, Kan., in 2005, some of his peers wondered whether his career was in eclipse.

In asking that nettlesome question four years ago — "Tell me how this ends" — Petraeus alluded to the advice supposedly given President Dwight Eisenhower in the mid-1950s when he asked what it would take for the U.S. military to save the beleaguered French colonial empire in war-torn Vietnam: "Eight years and eight divisions."

With only ten divisions now in the U.S. Army, and the American public's patience ebbing, Petraeus recently acknowledged that such a prescription is not likely to be any more acceptable today than it was in the 1950s.

Conrad Crane, a West Point classmate of Petraeus's who last year helped him write the new counterinsurgency manual, said: "There have been situations in our history where American generals were given tough problems to resolve, like Lincoln grabbing U.S. Grant in 1864. Those situations have all demanded steadfastness, fortitude, initiative and creativity. It will take all those traits in Baghdad.

"We've got a big problem," Crane added. "He's the right guy to fix it. If anybody can fix this, he can."

CAN PETRAEUS LEAD U.S. TO VICTORY?

/ General may be military's best -- and last -- hope in Iraq

Newspaper article Published Sunday, April 15, 2007

U.S. Commander in General David Petraeus gestures after attending a graduation ceremony for Special Operations forces in Baghdad March 29, 2007. Prime Minister Nuri al-Maliki and Petraeus attended a graduation ceremony for Special Operations forces in Baghdad

When hopeful Americans talk about Gen. David Petraeus, the new top U.S. military commander in Iraq, their thoughts turn wistfully to military heroes of yore.

He is the Ulysses S. Grant of the Bush administration, the general who can deliver a victory in a seemingly hopeless campaign. He is the modern-day Gen. William T. Sherman, a visionary tactician whose effort to secure Baghdad will be as pivotal to the American success in Iraq as the march through Atlanta was to the Union's triumph in the Civil War. He is "the closest thing the

Army has to its own Lawrence of Arabia," wrote Esquire magazine, evoking the British officer who helped the Arabs overthrow Ottoman dominion.

Petraeus may be Washington's best bet to lead U.S. troops in their latest attempt to pacify Iraq. His Princeton doctorate in international relations, his authorship last year of the military's counterinsurgency doctrine, and his success -- albeit temporary -- in bringing post-invasion stability to the northern Iraqi city of Mosul in 2003, when he commanded the 101st Airborne Division, distinguish Petraeus as the ultimate warrior-scholar. He wrote his doctoral thesis on the lessons learned in Vietnam, served in Bosnia after the civil war there and oversaw the initial reconstruction of Iraqi security forces. Many military officers, legislators and experts say he is probably the finest leader in the U.S. military today.

"He's the Gen. Grant of the surge," Sen. Lindsey Graham, R-S.C., said of Petraeus at the time of the general's confirmation hearings in January. "He's our last best chance as a military commander to bring about a change on the ground."

But even Petraeus' strongest supporters and friends agree that the general's impeccable credentials alone are not enough to help him accomplish the task Washington wants him to carry out: extinguish sectarian and anti-American violence, alleviate the social mistrust that grows deeper with every suicide bombing, and, eventually, help Iraq's elected government attain credibility among its people and establish a safe and democratic state.

"It does help if you have a good general (but) ultimately, it's not a question of how good he is," said Vali Nasr, professor of national security studies at the Naval Postgraduate School in Monterey.

"There are too many variables and a lot of unknowns out there," agreed Conrad Crane, director of the U.S. Army Military History Institute who went to West Point with Petraeus and helped him write the counterinsurgency manual.

On the surface, Petraeus' approach to solving the problem of Iraq is clear: Providing security in Baghdad will create a period of calm that Iraqi politicians can use to negotiate a better, safer Iraq. Then, American troops can go home.

"You secure Baghdad -- you win the country. You don't -- you won't," said Victor Davis Hanson, a historian at the Hoover Institution at Stanford University who has compared Petraeus to Sherman.

But this strategy presupposes it is possible to stop the violence long enough to create a window of quiet for Iraqi politicians to negotiate a power-sharing agreement that would appease Sunnis and Shiites alike -- and that should such a window be created, Iraqi politicians actually will take advantage of it, said Barry Posen, who taught Petraeus at Princeton in the mid-1980s and has remained friends with the general. Either outcome is unlikely, Posen and several other experts warn.

"I'm skeptical that David could even produce much of a window," said Posen, who heads the security studies program at the Massachusetts Institute of Technology. "But even if (he) does, there still is the question of will this window for politicians be used by these politicians?"

So far, in step with his counterinsurgency manual, Petraeus has asked for at least 21,500 additional troops to be sent to Iraq to implement the so-called Baghdad Security Plan, which puts more U.S. and Iraqi forces inside Baghdad neighborhoods in an effort to protect residents from insurgents and sectarian militias and pave the way for economic and political security.

But this textbook approach may not be enough to confront the reality, Crane said. "This may be the most complex conflict that we have ever faced," he said. "It's a whole maze of enemies that we face there, there are a lot of different conflicts going on."

Sectarian militias have metastasized into every neighborhood and infiltrated Iraq's U.S.-trained and Shiite-dominated security forces, which the populist Shiite cleric Muqtada al-Sadr is now urging to fight Americans. Sunni insurgents have learned to melt away from areas where the U.S. military is present, shifting the violence to places where coalition troops have less control. An example of the militants' ability to deliver unexpected and devastating attacks was the truck bomb that shook Tal Afar on March 27, killing at least 152 people and wounding hundreds more in the northern city the Bush administration once touted as a symbol of success. It was the deadliest bomb since the beginning of the war.

Even with additional troops, "We only control what we stand on," said retired Col. Douglas Macgregor, an adviser on military reform to the Center for Defense Information, an independent think tank in Washington. "Whenever you bring a large concentration of American forces, the Sunni insurgents or Shiite (militias) just move to a different location."

To get a better hold on territory, the new counterinsurgency field manual prescribes a ratio of 25 soldiers per 1,000 residents -- or 120,000 people for security forces in Baghdad alone. But even after the 21,500 additional American troops are deployed, Petraeus will still have a security force of only 85,000 in Baghdad, and that will include Iraqi security forces, whose preparedness and allegiance are questionable.

Petraeus, who has acknowledged the shortfall, hopes political negotiations will make up for it -- in line with the manual, which states that "some of the best weapons do not shoot."

"There is no military solution to a problem like that in Iraq," Petraeus told a news conference last month. "Military action is necessary to help improve security ... but it is not sufficient. There needs to be a political aspect."

This approach calls for an active "diplomatic surge," but this is not happening, Nasr said. "There is still no viable political track in Iraq," he said.

Washington continues to refuse to negotiate with Iran and Syria, Iraq's neighbors that the Bush administration has repeatedly accused of contributing to violence. The State Department has trouble filling civilian slots on the reconstruction teams it is sending to Iraq. And there are not enough diplomats shuttling between Iraq's Sunnis and Shiites to prepare them -- when and if Petraeus' security plan succeeds -- to seize upon the opportunity to negotiate a safer, better Iraq.

"You're asking David to make a heroic effort to create a window that doesn't have a very high probability of being used," Posen said.

Such strategy had a better chance of success at the beginning of the war, when Petraeus, then a major general, commanded the 101st Airborne Division in Mosul. His troops accompanied their house-to-house searches with community projects and constant negotiations with tribal chiefs. Such tactics helped the soldiers kill Saddam Hussein's sons and bring relative peace to the area.

But if there was another lesson to be learned from that experience, it was how quickly the calm disintegrated after the 101st went home and was replaced with another unit. By the end of 2004, insurgents took over most of Mosul, burning down police stations and prompting Americans to evacuate one of their bases before U.S. troops fought to regain control of the city in November 2004. Corpses of police officers executed by insurgents lay in the streets. That year, Petraeus presided over the effort to build Iraq's security forces -- which became permeated by Shiite militias who use their status to carry out reprisal killings.

"The control you have is illusory," Posen said. "There are going to be more surprises, intricacies I'm not sure anyone understands."

During the 2003 invasion, Petraeus asked a Washington Post reporter covering his division: "Tell me how this ends." Since then, fear and bloodshed have drenched Iraq, splitting the country along sectarian and ethnic lines, forcing at least 3 million Iraqis to flee, and killing, according to some estimates, hundreds of thousands of others. Even if the United States, its allies and Iraq's neighbors stepped up diplomatic activity in Iraq, the war-torn country may be too far gone to achieve the "happy ending in Iraq of the kind that the president talks about: Iraq that governs itself, protects itself, sustains itself ... a unified federal Iraq, democratic Iraq," Posen said.

"Four years into this war there's a lot more hope that's been lost by various Iraqis" to try to maintain Iraq as a unified nation, said Michael O'Hanlon, a friend of Petraeus and a senior fellow in foreign policy studies at the Brookings Institution in Washington.

More likely, not Petraeus but "the next American commander may be poised for success, because the next American commander will be the one negotiating a partitioning of Iraq" along sectarian and ethnic lines, said O'Hanlon, who attended graduate school with the general.

"You probably got the right guy four years into it, but can you really overcome the difficulties that we've created for the previous 48 months? Is he too little, too late?" O'Hanlon asked. "I have a sense that that could be the case."

U.S. Army Gen. David H. Petraeus, the commander of Multi-National Force – Iraq, briefs reporters at the Pentagon April 26, 2007, on his view of the current military situation in Iraq.

After taking command of MNF-I on February 10, 2007, Petraeus inspected U.S. and Iraqi units all over Iraq, visiting outposts in greater Baghdad, Tikrit, Baquba, Ramadi, Mosul, Kirkuk, Bayji, Samarra, Basrah and as far west as al-Hit and Al Qaim. In April 2007, Petraeus made his first visit to Washington as MNF-I Commander, reporting to President Bush and Congress on the progress of the "surge" and the overall situation in Iraq. During this visit he met privately with members of Congress and reportedly argued against setting a timetable for U.S. troop withdrawal from Iraq.

By late May 2007, Congress did not impose any timetables in war funding legislation for troop withdrawal. The enacted legislation did mandate that Petraeus and U.S. Ambassador to Iraq, Ryan Crocker, deliver a report to Congress by September 15, 2007, detailing their assessment of the military, economic and political situation of Iraq.

In June 2007, Petraeus stated in an interview that there were "astonishing signs of normalcy" in Baghdad, and this comment drew criticism from Senate majority leader Harry Reid. In the same interview, however, Petraeus stated that "many problems remain" and he noted the need to help the Iraqis "stitch back together the fabric of society that was torn during the height of sectarian violence" in late 2006. Petraeus also warned that he expected that the situation in Iraq would require the continued deployment of the elevated troop level of more than 150,000 beyond September 2007; he also stated that U.S. involvement in Iraq could last years afterward. These statements are representative of the fact that throughout their time in Iraq, Petraeus and Crocker remained circumspect and refused to classify themselves as optimists or pessimists, noting, instead, that they were realists and that the reality in Iraq was very hard. They also repeatedly emphasized the importance of forthright reports and an unvarnished approach. "Indeed, Petraeus' realistic approach and assessments were lauded during the McLaughlin Group's 2008 Year-End

Awards, when Monica Crowley nominated Petraeus for the most honest person of the year, stating, "..He spoke about the great successes of the surge in Iraq, but he always tempered it, never sugar-coated it."

Multi-National Force –
Iraq (summer and fall 2007)

In July 2007, the White House submitted to Congress the interim report on Iraq, which stated that coalition forces had made satisfactory progress on 6 of 18 benchmarks set by Congress. On September 7, 2007, in a letter addressed to the troops he was commanding, Petraeus wrote that much military progress had been made, but that the national level political progress that was hoped for had not been achieved. Petraeus' Report to Congress on the Situation in Iraq was delivered to Congress on September 10, 2007.

Here is a copy of that report

I have included the pictures (slides) in with the report to assist on following the topic.

Multi-National Force-Iraq

Charts to accompany the testimony of GEN David H. Petraeus

8-9 April 2008

Report to Congress on the Situation in Iraq

General David H. Petraeus

Commander, Multi-National Force–Iraq

8-9 April 2008

Mr. Chairman, Ranking Member, Members of the Committee, thank you for the opportunity to provide an update on the security situation in Iraq and to discuss the recommendations I recently provided to my chain of command.

Since Ambassador Crocker and I appeared before you seven months ago, there has been significant but uneven security progress in Iraq. Since September, levels of violence and civilian deaths have been reduced substantially, Al Qaeda-Iraq and a number of other extremist elements have been dealt serious blows, the capabilities of Iraqi Security Force elements have grown, and there has been noteworthy involvement of local Iraqis in local security. Nonetheless, the situation in certain areas is still unsatisfactory and innumerable challenges remain. Moreover, as events in the past two weeks have reminded us and as I have repeatedly cautioned, the progress made since last spring is fragile and reversible. Still, security in Iraq is better than it was when Ambassador Crocker and I reported to you last September, and it is significantly better than it was 15 months ago when Iraq was on the brink of civil war and the decision was made to deploy additional US forces to Iraq.

A number of factors have contributed to the progress that has been made. First, of course, has been the impact of increased numbers of Coalition and Iraqi Forces. You are well aware of the U.S. surge. Less recognized is that Iraq has also conducted a surge, adding well over 100,000 additional soldiers and police to the ranks of its security forces in 2007 and slowly increasing its capability to deploy and employ these forces.

A second factor has been the employment of Coalition and Iraqi Forces in the conduct of counterinsurgency operations across the country, deployed together to safeguard the Iraqi people, to pursue Al Qaeda-Iraq, to combat criminals and militia extremists, to foster local reconciliation, and to enable political and economic progress.

Another important factor has been the attitudinal shift among certain elements of the Iraqi population. Since the first Sunni "Awakening" in late 2006, Sunni communities in Iraq increasingly have rejected AQI's indiscriminate violence and extremist ideology. These communities also recognized that they could not share in Iraq's bounty if they didn't participate in the political arena. Over time, Awakenings have prompted tens of thousands of Iraqis—some, former insurgents—to contribute to local security as so-called "Sons of Iraq." With their assistance and with relentless pursuit of Al Qaeda-Iraq, the threat posed by AQI—while still lethal and substantial—has been reduced significantly.

The recent flare-up in Basrah, southern Iraq, and Baghdad underscored the importance of the ceasefire declared by Moqtada al-Sadr last fall as another factor in the overall reduction in violence. Recently, of course, some militia elements became active again. Though a Sadr standdown

order resolved the situation to a degree, the flare-up also highlighted the destructive role Iran has played in funding, training, arming, and directing the so-called Special Groups and generated renewed concern about Iran in the minds of many Iraqi leaders. Unchecked, the Special Groups pose the greatest long-term threat to the viability of a democratic Iraq.

As we look to the future, our task together with our Iraqi partners will be to build on the progress achieved and to deal with the many challenges that remain. I do believe that we can do this while continuing the ongoing drawdown of the surge forces.

The Nature of the Conflict

In September, I described the fundamental nature of the conflict in Iraq as a competition among ethnic and sectarian communities for power and resources. This competition continues, influenced heavily by outside actors, and its resolution remains the key to producing long-term stability in Iraq.

Various elements push Iraq's ethno-sectarian competition toward violence. Terrorists, insurgents, militia extremists, and criminal gangs pose significant threats. Al Qaeda's senior leaders, who still view Iraq as the central front in their global strategy, send funding, direction, and foreign fighters to Iraq. Actions by neighboring states compound Iraq's challenges. Syria has taken some steps to reduce the flow of foreign fighters through its territory, but not enough to shut down the key network that supports AQI. And Iran has fueled the violence in a particularly damaging way, through its lethal support to the Special Groups. Finally, insufficient Iraqi governmental capacity, lingering sectarian mistrust, and corruption add to Iraq's problems. These challenges and recent weeks' violence notwithstanding, Iraq's ethno-sectarian competition in many areas is now taking place more through debate and less through violence. In fact, the recent escalation of violence in Baghdad and southern Iraq was dealt with temporarily, at least, by most parties acknowledging that the rational way ahead is political dialogue rather than street fighting.

Current Situation and Trends

As I stated at the outset, though Iraq obviously remains a violent country, we do see progress in the security arena.

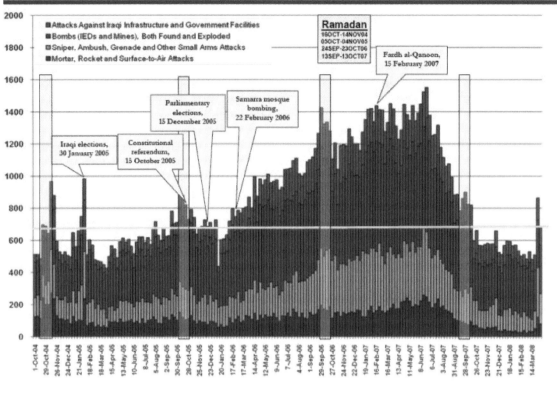

As this chart [Slide 1] illustrates, for nearly six months, security incidents have been at a level not seen since early-to-mid-2005, though the level did spike in recent weeks as a result of the violence in Basrah and Baghdad. The level of incidents has, however, begun to turn down again, though the period ahead will be a sensitive one.

As our primary mission is to help protect the population, we closely monitor the number of Iraqi civilians killed due to violence.

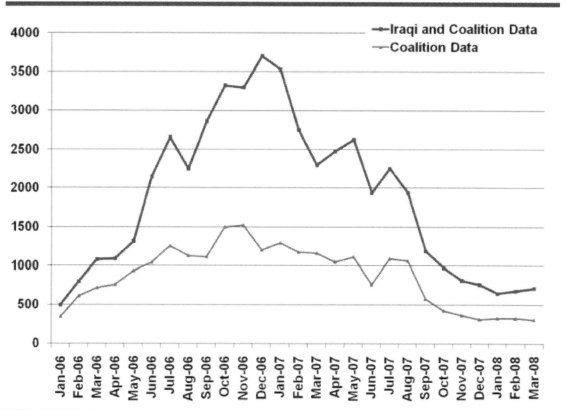

As this chart [Slide 2] reflects, civilian deaths have decreased over the past year to a level not seen since the February 2006 Samarra Mosque bombing that set off the cycle of sectarian violence that tore the very fabric of Iraqi society in 2006 and early 2007. This chart also reflects our increasing use of Iraqi-provided reports, with the top line reflecting Coalition and Iraqi data and the bottom line reflecting Coalition-confirmed data only. No matter which data is used, civilian deaths due to violence have been reduced significantly, though more work clearly needs to be done.

Ethno-sectarian violence is a particular concern in Iraq, as it is a cancer that continues to spread if left unchecked.

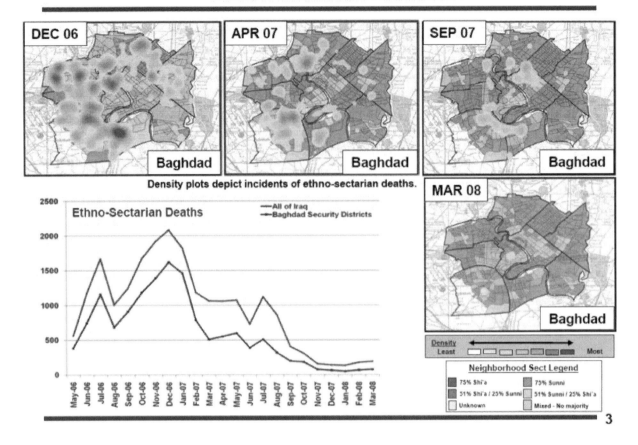

As the box on the bottom left of this chart [Slide 3] shows, the number of deaths due to ethno-sectarian violence has fallen since we testified last September. A big factor has been the reduction of ethno-sectarian violence in Baghdad, density plots for which are shown in the boxes depicting Iraq's capital over time. Some of this decrease is, to be sure, due to sectarian hardening of certain Baghdad neighborhoods; however, that is only a partial explanation as countless sectarian fault lines and numerous mixed neighborhoods still exist in Baghdad and elsewhere. In fact, Coalition and Iraqi Forces have focused along the fault lines to reduce the violence and enable Sunni and Shia leaders to begin the long process of healing in their local communities.

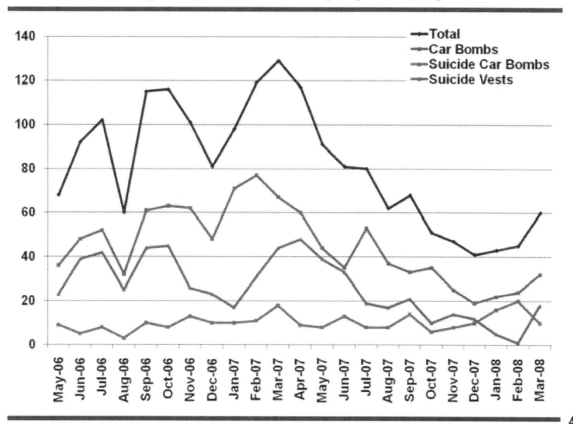

As this next chart [Slide 4] shows, even though the number of high profile attacks increased in March as AQI lashed out, the current level of such attacks remains far below its height a year ago. Moreover, as we have helped improve security and focused on enemy networks, we have seen a decrease in the effectiveness of such attacks. The number of deaths due to ethno-sectarian violence, in particular, has remained relatively low, illustrating the enemy's inability to date to re-ignite the cycle of ethno-sectarian violence.

The emergence of Iraqi volunteers helping to secure their local communities has been an important development.

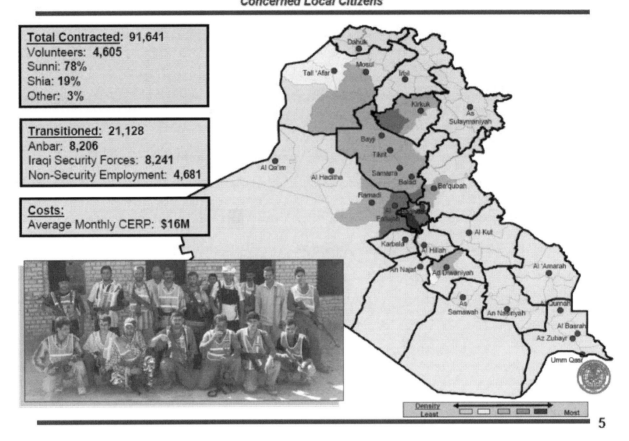

As this chart [Slide 5] depicts, there are now over 91,000 Sons of Iraq—Shia as well as Sunni—under contract to help Coalition and Iraqi Forces protect their neighborhoods and secure infrastructure and roads. These volunteers have contributed significantly in various areas, and the savings in vehicles not lost because of reduced violence—not to mention the priceless lives saved—have far outweighed the cost of their monthly contracts.

Sons of Iraq have also contributed to the discovery of improvised explosive devices and weapons and explosives caches.

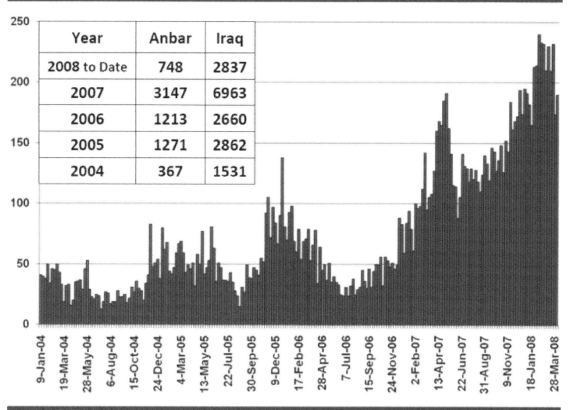

As this next chart [Slide 6] shows, in fact, we have already found more caches in 2008 than we found in all of 2006. Given the importance of the Sons of Iraq, we are working closely with the Iraqi Government to transition them into the Iraqi Security Forces or other forms of employment, and over 21,000 have already been accepted into the Police or Army or other government jobs. This process has been slow, but it is taking place, and we will continue to monitor it carefully.

Al Qaeda also recognizes the significance of the Sons of Iraq, and AQI elements have targeted them repeatedly. However, these attacks—in addition to AQI's use of women, children, and the handicapped as suicide bombers—have further alienated AQI from the Iraqi people. And the tenacious pursuit of AQI, together with AQI's loss of local support in many areas, has substantially reduced its capability, numbers, and freedom of movement.

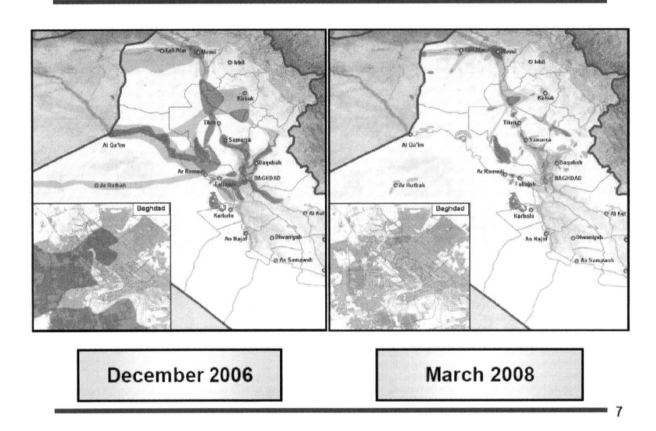

This chart [Slide 7] displays the cumulative effect of the effort against AQI and its insurgent allies. As you can see, we have reduced considerably the areas in which AQI enjoys support and sanctuary, though there clearly is more to be done.

Having noted that progress, AQI is still capable of lethal attacks, and we must maintain relentless pressure on the organization, on the networks outside Iraq that support it, and on the resource flows that sustain it.

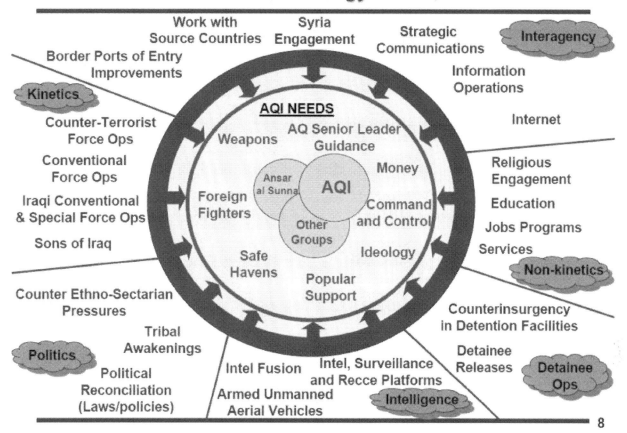

This chart [Slide 8] lays out the comprehensive strategy that we, the Iraqis, and our interagency and international partners are employing to reduce what AQI needs. As you can see, defeating Al Qaeda in Iraq requires not just actions by our elite counter-terrorist forces, but also major operations by Coalition and Iraqi conventional forces, a sophisticated intelligence effort, political reconciliation, economic and social programs, information operations initiatives, diplomatic activity, the employment of counterinsurgency principles in detainee operations, and many other actions. Related to this effort, I applaud Congress' support for additional intelligence, surveillance, and reconnaissance assets in the upcoming Supplemental, as ISR is vital to the success of our operations in Iraq and elsewhere.

As we combat AQI, we must remember that doing so not only reduces a major source of instability in Iraq; it also weakens an organization that Al Qaeda's senior leaders view as a tool to spread its influence and foment regional instability. Usama bin Ladin and Ayman al-Zawahiri have consistently advocated exploiting the situation in Iraq, and we have also seen AQI involved in destabilizing activities in the wider Mid-east region.

Together with the Iraqi Security Forces, we have also focused on the Special Groups. These elements are funded, trained, armed, and directed by Iran's Qods Force, with help from Lebanese Hezbollah. It was these groups that launched Iranian rockets and mortar rounds at Iraq's seat of government two weeks ago, causing loss of innocent life and fear in the capital, and requiring Iraqi and Coalition actions in response. Iraqi and Coalition leaders have repeatedly noted their desire that Iran live up to promises made by President Ahmedinajad and other senior Iranian leaders to stop their support for the Special Groups. However, nefarious activities by the Qods Force have continued, and Iraqi leaders now clearly recognize the threat they pose to Iraq. We should all watch Iranian actions closely in the weeks and months ahead, as they will show the kind of relationship Iran wishes to have with its neighbor and the character of future Iranian involvement in Iraq.

Iraqi Security Forces

The Iraqi Security Forces have continued to develop since September, and we have transferred responsibilities to Iraqi Forces as their capabilities and the conditions on the ground have permitted.

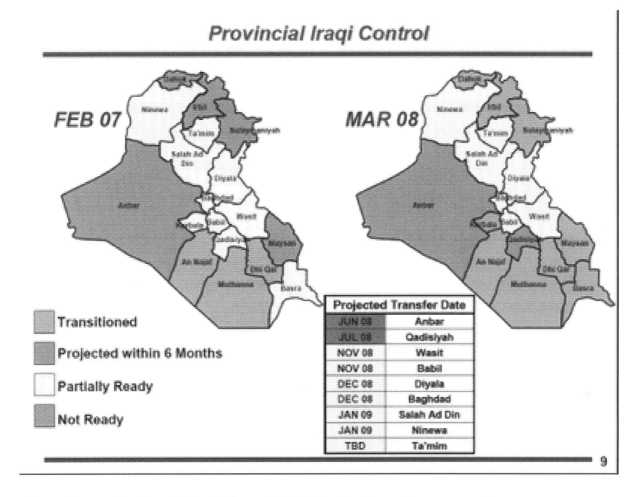

Currently, as this chart [Slide 9] shows, half of Iraq's 18 provinces are under provincial Iraqi control. Many of these provinces—not just the successful provinces in the Kurdish Regional Government area, but also a number of southern provinces—have done well. Challenges have emerged in some others, including, of course, Basrah. Nonetheless, this process will continue, and we expect Anbar and Qadisiyah Provinces to transition in the months ahead. Iraqi Forces have grown significantly since September, and over 540,000 individuals now serve in the Iraqi Security Forces.

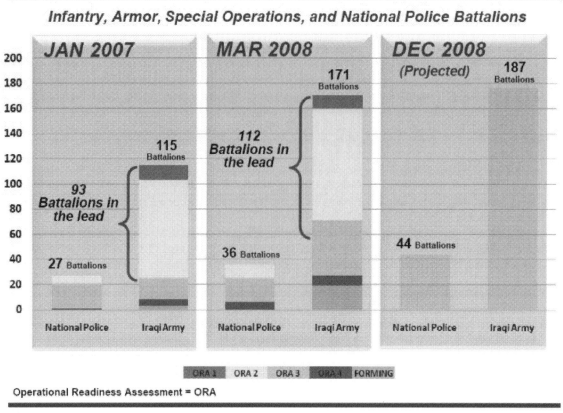

The number of combat battalions capable of taking the lead in operations, albeit with some Coalition support, has grown to well over 100 [Slide 10]. These units are bearing an increasing share of the burden, as evidenced by the fact that Iraqi Security Force losses have recently been three times our own. We will, of course, conduct careful after action reviews with our Iraqi partners in the wake of recent operations, as there were units and leaders found wanting in some cases, and some of our assessments may be downgraded as a result. Nonetheless, the performance of many units was solid, especially once they got their footing and gained a degree of confidence, and certain Iraqi elements proved quite capable. Underpinning the advances of the past year have been improvements in Iraq's security institutions. An increasingly robust Iraqi-run training base enabled the Iraqi Security Forces to grow by over 133,000 soldiers and police over the past 16 months. And the still-expanding training base is expected to generate an additional 50,000 Iraqi soldiers and 16 Army and Special Operations battalions throughout the rest of 2008, along with over 23,000 police and 8 National Police battalions.

Additionally, Iraq's security ministries are steadily improving their ability to execute their budgets.

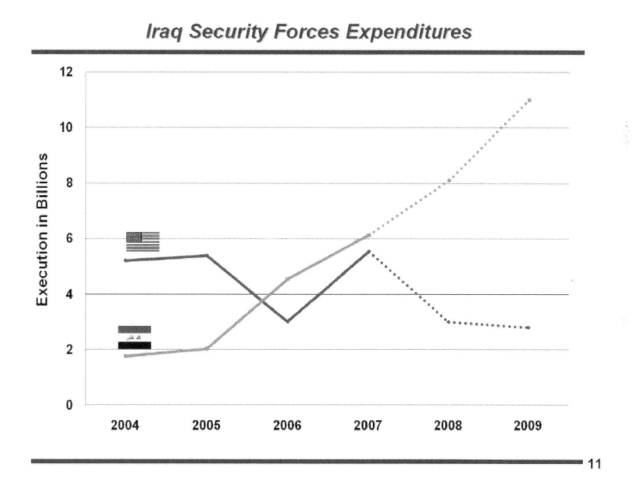

As this chart [Slide 11] shows, in 2007, as in 2006, Iraq's security ministries spent more on their forces than the United States provided through the Iraqi Security Forces Fund (ISFF). We anticipate that Iraq will spend over $8 billion on security this year and $11 billion next year, and this projection enabled us recently to reduce significantly our Iraqi Security Forces Fund request for fiscal year 2009 from $5.1 billion to $2.8 billion.

While improved, Iraqi Security Forces are not yet ready to defend Iraq or maintain security throughout the country on their own. Recent operations in Basrah highlight improvements in the ability of the Iraqi Security Forces to deploy substantial numbers of units, supplies, and replacements on very short notice; they certainly could not have deployed a division's worth of Army and Police units on such short notice a year ago. On the other hand, the recent operations also underscored the considerable work still to be done in the areas of logistics, force enablers, staff development, and command and control.

We also continue to help Iraq through the U.S. Foreign Military Sales program. As of March 2008, the Iraqi government has purchased over $2 billion worth of equipment and services of American origin through FMS. Since September, and with your encouragement of the organizations in the FMS process, delivery has improved as the FMS system has strived to support urgent wartime requirements. On a related note, I would ask that Congress consider restoring funding for the International Military Education and Training Program, which supports education for mid- and senior-level Iraqi military and civilian leaders and is an important component of the development of the leaders Iraq will need in the future.

Upcoming Challenges

While security has improved in many areas and the Iraqi Security Forces are shouldering more of the load, the situation in Iraq remains exceedingly complex and challenging. Iraq could face a resurgence of AQI or additional Shia groups could violate Moqtada al-Sadr's cease-fire order and return to violence. External actors, like Iran, could stoke violence within Iraq, and actions by other neighbors could undermine the security situation as well.

Other challenges result, paradoxically, from improved security, which has provided opportunities for political and economic progress and improved services at the local, provincial, and national levels. But the improvements have also created expectations that progress will continue. In the coming months, Iraq's leaders must strengthen governmental capacity, execute budgets, pass additional legislation, conduct provincial elections, carry out a census, determine the status of disputed territories, and resettle internally displaced persons and refugees. These tasks would challenge any government, much less a still developing government tested by war.

The Commander's Emergency Response Program, the State Department's Quick Response Fund, and USAID programs enable us to help Iraq deal with its challenges. To that end, I respectfully ask that you provide us by June the additional CERP funds requested in the Supplemental. These funds have an enormous impact. As I noted earlier, the salaries paid to the Sons of Iraq alone cost far less than the cost savings in vehicles not lost due to the enhanced security in local communities. Encouragingly, the Iraqi government recently allocated $300 million for us to manage as "Iraqi CERP" to perform projects for their people, while building their own capacity to do so. The Iraqi government has also committed $163 million to gradually assume Sons of Iraq contracts, $510 million for small business loans, and $196 million for a Joint Training, Education, and Reintegration Program. The Iraqi government pledges to provide more as they execute the budget passed two months ago. Nonetheless, it is hugely important to have our resources continue, even as Iraqi funding begins to outstrip ours.

Recommendations

Last month I provided my chain of command recommendations for the way ahead in Iraq. During that process, I noted the objective of retaining and building on our hard-fought security gains while we draw down to the pre-surge level of 15 brigade combat teams. I emphasized the need to continue work with our Iraqi partners to secure the population and to transition responsibilities to the Iraqis as quickly as conditions permit, but without jeopardizing the security gains that have been made.

As in September, my recommendations are informed by operational and strategic considerations. The operational considerations include recognition that:

• the military surge has achieved progress, but that the progress is reversible;

• Iraqi Security Forces have strengthened their capabilities but still must grow further;

• the provincial elections in the fall, refugee returns, detainee releases, and efforts to resolve provincial boundary disputes and Article 140 issues will be very challenging;

• the transition of Sons of Iraq into the Iraqi Security Forces or other pursuits will require time and careful monitoring;

• withdrawing too many forces too quickly could jeopardize the progress of the past year; and

• performing the necessary tasks in Iraq will require sizable conventional forces as well as special operations forces and advisor teams.

The strategic considerations include recognition that:

- the strain on the US military, especially on its ground forces, has been considerable;

- a number of the security challenges inside Iraq are also related to significant regional and global threats; and

- a failed state in Iraq would pose serious consequences for the greater fight against Al Qaeda, for regional stability, for the already existing humanitarian crisis in Iraq, and for the effort to counter malign Iranian influence.

After weighing these factors, I recommended to my chain of command that we continue the drawdown of the surge combat forces and that, upon the withdrawal of the last surge brigade combat team in July, we undertake a 45-day period of consolidation and evaluation. At the end of that period, we will commence a process of assessment to examine the conditions on the ground and, over time, determine when we can make recommendations for further reductions. This process will be continuous, with recommendations for further reductions made as conditions permit. This approach does not allow establishment of a set withdrawal timetable; however, it does provide the flexibility those of us on the ground need to preserve the still fragile security gains our troopers have fought so hard and sacrificed so much to achieve.

With this approach, the security achievements of 2007 and early 2008 can form a foundation for the gradual establishment of sustainable security in Iraq. This is not only important to the 27 million citizens of Iraq; it is also vitally important to those in the Gulf region, to the citizens of the United States, and to the global community. It clearly is in our national interest to help Iraq prevent the resurgence of Al Qaeda in the heart of the Arab world, to help Iraq resist Iranian encroachment on its sovereignty, to avoid renewed ethno-sectarian violence that could spill over

Iraq's borders and make the existing refugee crisis even worse, and to enable Iraq to expand its role in the regional and global economies.

Closing Comments

In closing, I want to comment briefly on those serving our Nation in Iraq. We have asked a great deal of them and of their families, and they have made enormous sacrifices. My keen personal awareness of the strain on them and on the force as a whole has been an important factor in my recommendations.

The Congress, the Executive Branch, and our fellow citizens have done an enormous amount to support our troopers and their loved ones, and all of us are grateful for that. Nothing means more to those in harm's way than the knowledge that their country appreciates their sacrifices and those of their families.

Indeed, all Americans should take great pride in the men and women serving our Nation in Iraq and in the courage, determination, resilience, and initiative they demonstrate each and every day. It remains the greatest of honors to soldier with them.

Thank you very much.

On August 15, 2007, the *Los Angeles Times* stated that, according to unnamed administration officials, the report "would actually be written by the White House, with inputs from officials throughout the government". However, Petraeus declared in his testimony to Congress that "I wrote this testimony myself." He further elaborated that his testimony to Congress "has not been cleared by, nor shared with, anyone in the Pentagon, the White House, or Congress".

GEN Petraeus with LTG Odierno (left), President Bush (center), SecDef Gates, and Sec State Rice (right) at Al Asad Airbase in September 2007

In his September Congressional testimony, Petraeus stated that "As a bottom line up front, the military objectives of the surge are, in large measure, being met." He cited numerous factors for this progress, to include the fact that Coalition and Iraqi Forces had dealt significant blows to Al-Qaeda Iraq and had disrupted Shia militias, that ethno-sectarian violence had been reduced, and that the tribal rejection of Al-Qaeda had spread from Anbar Province to numerous other locations across Iraq. Based on this progress and additional progress expected to be achieved, Petraeus recommended drawing down the surge forces from Iraq and gradually transitioning increased responsibilities to Iraqi Forces, as their capabilities and conditions on the ground permitted.

Democratic Senate Majority Leader Harry Reid of Nevada argued Petraeus' "plan is just more of the same" and "is neither a drawdown nor a change in mission that we need". Democratic Representative Robert Wexler of Florida accused Petraeus of "cherry-picking statistics" and "massaging information". Chairman of the House Foreign Affairs Committee Tom Lantos of California called the General and U.S. Ambassador to Iraq Ryan Crocker "Two of our nation's most capable public servants" and said Democrats feel "esteem for their professionalism". He also said that "We can no longer take their assertions on Iraq at face value"; concluding, "We need to get out of Iraq, for that country's sake as well as our own."

Republican Presidential candidate Duncan Hunter called the report "a candid, independent assessment given with integrity". Republican Senator Jon Kyl of Arizona stated that "I commend General Petraeus for his honest and forthright assessment of the situation in Iraq." Anti-war Republican Senator Chuck Hagel of Nebraska criticized the report while praising Petraeus, saying "It's not your fault, general... It's not Ambassador Crocker's fault. It's this administration's fault." A *USA Today*/Gallup poll taken after Petraeus' report to Congress showed virtually no change in public opinion toward the war. A Pew Research Center survey found that most Americans who have heard about the report approve of Petraeus' recommendations.

On September 20, the Senate passed an amendment by Republican John Cornyn III of Texas designed to "strongly condemn personal attacks on the honor and integrity of General Petraeus". Cornyn drafted the amendment in response to a controversial full-page ad by the liberal group Moveon.org in the September 10, 2007, edition of *The New York Times*. All forty-nine Republican Senators and twenty-two Democratic Senators voted in support. The House passed a similar resolution by a 341–79 vote on September 26.

MoveOn.org ad controversy

The **MoveOn.org ad controversy** began when the US anti-war liberal advocacy group MoveOn.org published a full-page ad in *The New York Times* on September 10, 2007 accusing General David H. Petraeus of "cooking the books for the White House". The ad also labeled him "General Betray Us". The organization created the ad in response to Petraeus' Report to Congress on the Situation in Iraq. MoveOn hosted pages on its website about the ad and their reasons behind it from 2007 to June 23, 2010. On June 23, 2010, after President Obama nominated General Petraeus to be the new top U.S. and NATO commander in Afghanistan (taking over the position from retiring General Stanley McChrystal), MoveOn erased these webpages and any reference to them from its website.

Arguments

The ad argued:

> "Every independent report on the ground situation in Iraq shows that the surge strategy has failed."

>> The group later cited the GAO, NIE, and Jones reports published for Congress around the same time as Petraeus' report. *USA Today* compared the four reports' findings. *The New York Times* also did so. The group referred to an Associated Press study finding that the civilian death toll in August 2007 was the second highest since the surge began. The study found as well that "monthly death tolls began to decline after the new security plan was launched" and that "Deaths went down in Baghdad during August". The group also referred to a *Los Angeles Times* article stating that "the U.S. troop increase has had little effect."

> "Yet the General claims a reduction in violence. That's because, according to the New York Times, the Pentagon has adopted a bizarre formula for keeping tabs on violence. For example, deaths by car bombs don't count."

>> The group later referred to an editorial by liberal columnist Paul Krugman. *The Washington Post* has stated that Petraeus' report included data about car bombs.

> "The Washington Post reported that assassinations only count if you're shot in the back of the head -- not the front."

>> *The Washington Post* article anonymously quoted a senior intelligence official in Washington commenting on U.S. military data. The official stated that "If a bullet went through the back of the head, it's sectarian" but that "If it went through the front, it's criminal." According to *The Washington Post*, the MNF-I says that they make no distinction among the possible points of impact on the head.

"According to news reports, there have been more civilian deaths and more American soldier deaths in the past three months than in any other summer we've been there."

> The group later cited an Associated Press story stating that "This year's U.S. troop buildup has succeeded in bringing violence in Baghdad down from peak levels, but the death toll from sectarian attacks around the country is running nearly double the pace from a year ago." The story also stated that "The U.S. military did not get all the additional American forces into Iraq until June 15, so it would be premature to draw a final statistical picture of the effect of the added troops." The group also cited an NPR article quoting former Army Colonel Doug MacGregor calling Petraeus' statistics "an illusion created by the White House". The article concluded by stating that "So is the surge working? The short answer is that no one can know for certain because statistics only tell a small part of the story."

"We'll hear of neighborhoods where violence has decreased. But we won't hear that those neighborhoods have been ethnically cleansed."

> The group later cited a *Newsweek* story stating that "When Gen. David Petraeus goes before Congress next week to report on the progress of the surge, he may cite a decline in insurgent attacks in Baghdad as one marker of success. In fact, part of the reason behind the decline is how far the Shiite militias' cleansing of Baghdad has progressed: they've essentially won."

"Iraq is mired in an unwinnable religious civil war."

"General Petraeus has actually said American troops will need to stay in Iraq for as long as ten years."

> The group later referred to a statement by Democratic Congresswoman Jan Schakowsky. The nonpartisan website Factcheck.org criticized previous ads that state that Petraeus supports leaving troops in Iraq for ten more years because Petraeus had only said, during a BBC News interview, that "the average counter-insurgency is somewhere around a 9- or a 10- year endeavor" in reference to The Troubles in Northern Ireland.

In December 2007, *The Washington Post*'s "Fact Checker" stated that "While some of Petraeus's statistics are open to challenge, his claims about a general reduction in violence have been borne out over subsequent months. It now looks as if Petraeus was broadly right on this issue at least".

Based on the conditions on the ground, in October 2007, Petraeus and U.S. Ambassador to Iraq Ryan Crocker revised their campaign plan for Iraq. In recognition of the progress made against Al Qaeda Iraq, one of the major points would be "shifting the U.S. military effort to focus more on countering Shiite militias".

U.S. Ambassador to Iraq Ryan Crocker

Multi-National Force – Iraq (spring 2008)

On February 18, 2008, *USA Today* stated that "the U.S. effort has shown more success" and that, after the number of troops reached its peak in fall 2007, "U.S. deaths were at their lowest levels since the 2003 invasion, civilian casualties were down, and street life was resuming in Baghdad." In light of the significant reduction in violence and as the surge brigades began to redeploy without replacement, Petraeus characterized the progress as tenuous, fragile, and reversible and repeatedly reminded all involved that much work remains to be done. During an early February trip to Iraq, Defense Secretary Robert Gates endorsed the idea of a period of consolidation and evaluation upon completion of the withdrawal of surge brigades from Iraq.

Petraeus and Crocker continued these themes at their two full days of testimony before Congress on April 8 and 9th. During his opening statement, Petraeus stated that "there has been significant but uneven security progress in Iraq," while also noting that "the situation in certain areas is still unsatisfactory and that innumerable challenges remain" and that "the progress made since last spring is fragile and reversible." He also recommended a continuation of the drawdown of surge forces as well as a 45-day period of consolidation and evaluation after the final surge brigade has redeployed in late July. Analysts for *USA Today* and *The New York Times* stated that the hearings "lacked the suspense of last September's debate," but they did include sharp questioning as well as both skepticism and praise from various Congressional leaders.

In late May 2008, the Senate Armed Services Committee held nomination hearings for Petraeus and Lieutenant General Ray Odierno to lead United States Central Command and Multi-National Force-Iraq, respectively. During the hearings, Committee Chairman Carl Levin praised these two men, stating that "we owe Gen. Petraeus and Gen. Odierno a debt of gratitude for the commitment, determination and strength that they brought to their areas of responsibility. And regardless of how long the administration may choose to remain engaged in the strife in that country, our troops are better off with the leadership these two distinguished soldiers provide." During his opening statement, Petraeus discussed four principles that would guide his efforts if confirmed as CENTCOM Commander: seeking to strengthen international partnerships; taking a "whole of government" approach; pursuing comprehensive efforts and solutions; and, finally, both supporting efforts in Iraq and Afghanistan and ensuring readiness for possible contingency operations in the future. Petraeus also noted that during the week before his testimony, the number of security incidents in Iraq was the lowest in over four years. After Petraeus' return to Baghdad, and despite the continued drawdown of surge forces as well as recent Iraqi-led operations in places like Basrah, Mosul, and Baghdad, the number of security incidents in Iraq remained at their lowest level in over four years.

Multi-National Force – Iraq (summer and fall 2008)

Petraeus explains security improvements in Sadr City while giving an aerial tour of Baghdad to Senator Barack Obama, July 2008

In September 2008, Petraeus gave an interview to BBC News stating that he did not think using the term "victory" in describing the Iraq war was appropriate, saying "This is not the sort of struggle where you take a hill, plant the flag and go home to a victory parade... it's not war with a simple slogan."

Petraeus had discussed the term 'victory' before in March 2008, saying to NPR News that "an Iraq that is at peace with itself, at peace with its neighbors, that has a government that is representative of—and responsive to—its citizenry and is a contributing member of the global community" could arguably be called 'victory'. On the eve of his change of command, in September 2008, Petraeus stated that "I don't use terms like victory or defeat... I'm a realist, not an optimist or a pessimist. And the reality is that there has been significant progress but there are still serious challenges."

Change of command

Iraq Defense Minister Abdul Qadir presents a gift to Petraeus during a farewell ceremony in Baghdad on September 15, 2008.

On September 16, 2008, Petraeus formally gave over his command in Iraq to General Raymond T. Odierno in a government ceremony presided by Defense Secretary Robert Gates. During the ceremony, Gates stated that Petraeus "played a historic role" and created the "translation of a great strategy into a great success in very difficult circumstances". Gates also told Petraeus he believed "history will regard you as one of our nation's greatest battle captains."

He presented Petraeus with the Defense Distinguished Service Medal. At the event, Petraeus mentioned the difficulty in getting the Sons of Iraq absorbed in the central Government of Iraq and warned about future consequences if the effort stalls.

Defense Distinguished Service Medal

Indeed, when speaking of these and other challenges, Petraeus is the first to note that "the gains [achieved in Iraq] are tenuous and unlikely to survive without an American effort that outlasts his tenure". Even so, as Petraeus departed Iraq, it was clear to all that he was leaving a much different Iraq than the one that existed when he took command in February 2007. As described by Dexter Filkins, "violence has plummeted from its apocalyptic peaks, Iraqi leaders are asserting themselves, and streets that once seemed dead are flourishing with life." This is also illustrated by the Iraq Trends charts that the MNF-I produces weekly. The January 3, 2009, "Iraq Trends Chart" clearly depicts over time, the increases in incidents followed by the sharp decline as described by Dexter Filkens and others.

General Petraeus' critical role in Iraq has been widely acknowledged by commands of the coalition forces. In her introduction of Petraeus at the Baccalaureate ceremony for the Class of 2009, Princeton University President Shirley Tilghman described his accomplishments. While acknowledging that much remains to be accomplished in Iraq, Tilghman paid tribute to Petraeus' "leadership in rethinking American military strategy through his principles of counterinsurgency," which are, she said, "eliminating 'simplistic definitions of victory and defeat in favor of incremental and nuanced progress'."

Princeton University President Shirley Tilghman

Health problems

General Petraeus was diagnosed with early-stage prostate cancer in February 2009 and underwent two months of successful radiation treatment at Walter Reed Army Medical Center.[1] The diagnosis and treatment was not publicly disclosed until October 2009 because Petraeus and his family regarded his illness as a personal matter that did not interfere with the performance of his duties.

Gen. David Petraeus was diagnosed with prostate cancer in February.

He was diagnosed in February, his office said, and underwent two months of radiation treatment at Walter Reed Army Medical Center in Washington, D.C.

"My cancer was caught very early," Petraeus, 56, said in remarks released by his office. "I've had two PSA tests since completing treatment five months ago, and they've both been very positive. Surgery to remove the prostate was not an option due to plates/screws that were used to repair my pelvis after it was fractured in a parachuting accident."

PSA tests are blood tests performed to screen for prostate-specific antigens -- proteins produced by cells of the prostate. Higher levels of PSAs could signal prostate cancer or benign prostate conditions.

At an appearance Tuesday after news of the treatment was out, Petraeus made only a lighthearted comment about this health.

"With the CNN reports today, they're all just here to see if the guy's still alive or not," said Petraeus, joking about the camera crews recording his speech at the Association of the United States Army meeting in Washington. He did not comment further on his condition.

The treatment had "minimal impact on his work schedule as he was spending 4-5 days a week in Washington, D.C., for various policy reviews and other Pentagon activities at that time," the statement said.

Petraeus made at least one overseas trip during the radiation treatment.

He regarded his illness a personal matter and kept it largely private because it did not interfere with his duties, the statement said.

However, the president, vice president, secretaries of state and defense and the chairman of the Joint Chiefs of Staff were notified of Petraeus' condition, the statement said.

That's not even surprising. In 1991, then-Col. Petraeus was shot in the chest by accident during a live-fire training exercise at Fort Campbell and underwent an extremely painful pre-surgery procedure and then a lengthy surgery. Tom Ricks recounts what happened "less than a week later" when a restless Petraeus grew tired of his Fort Campbell recuperation and sought a discharge:

"That's impossible– you're not going home," the doctor said.

"Can I demonstrate to you the degree of my recovery?" asked Petraeus.

The doctor asked what he meant. "Just undo my tubes here," Petraeus said. "Don't worry, I'm not going to do anything to hurt myself, just undo my tubes." He got down on the floor and counted out 50 push-ups for the doctor, who then allowed him to leave the hospital.

That's a Chuck Norris move right there. The odds are clearly against cancer.

U.S. Central Command
(fall 2008 to summer 2010)

Petraeus set to perform coin toss for Super Bowl XLIII

January 30, 2009

WASHINGTON - From fighter jet flyovers to military performances at halftime shows, the National Football League and U.S. military have shared more than 40 years of Super Bowl history.

The tradition continues Feb. 1 in Tampa, Fla., during Super Bowl XLIII, with Gen. David H. Petraeus, commander of U.S. Central Command, performing the ceremonial coin toss for the Arizona Cardinals' and Pittsburgh Steelers' team captains.

"It is a privilege to represent our Soldiers, sailors, airmen, Marines and Coast Guardsmen in the coin-toss ceremony," Petraeus told American Forces Press Service today in an e-mail. "And it is an honor to thank the NFL commissioner and the teams and players for all that they have done in recent years to recognize the service of our troopers and their families."

The Air Force Thunderbirds aerial demonstration squadron is set for a pregame flyover, and an all-service U.S. Special Operations Command color guard is planned to present the nation's colors during the game's national anthem.

Air Force Tech Sgt. Holly Bracken will be on the field in the color guard formation, presenting the Air Force colors. She's privileged to represent her service and the military, she said, adding that it just wouldn't be a Super Bowl without military support.

"It's such an honor to go there and present the colors," said Bracken, who grew up near Pittsburgh rooting for the Steelers. "You can't have the presentation of the colors without [military] representation."

The NFL-military Super Bowl partnership stems from the first Air Force flyover in 1968 over Miami's Orange Bowl for Super Bowl II. Ever since, flyovers have become a staple of the Super Bowl, NFL spokesman Brian McCarthy said, citing military flyovers as "an unbelievable experience" to watch from the football field.

Since then, the military has supported flyovers for nearly every Super Bowl, he said. Also, military choirs have performed the pregame national anthem twice, with the U.S. Air Force Academy Chorale singing for Super Bowl VI in 1972, and a combined chorus from the U.S. Military Academy at West Point, the U.S. Naval Academy and the U.S. Coast Guard Academy singing for Super Bowl XXXIX in 2005.

The Marine Corps Silent Drill Platoon performed at halftime for Super Bowl VI in 1972, and the U.S. Air Force Band did the same in 1985 for Super Bowl XIX.

The military even has taken on its normal role as peacekeeper and protector for past Super Bowls, with the Florida Army National Guard taking part in security efforts in 2005 and 2007 along with other federal and state agencies.

"The NFL has had a longstanding tradition of supporting the military," NFL spokesman Brian McCarthy told American Forces Press Service during a phone interview. "We have a great appreciation for what the military does and feel honored to include the military in the Super Bowl."

Throughout the years, the Super Bowl has become one of the most highly rated televised events of the year. This year, Super Bowl XLIII will be broadcast to more than 230 countries to a potential worldwide audience of more than 1 billion viewers, including military members serving in Iraq and Afghanistan.

McCarthy said the NFL is working with NBC, which has the broadcast rights for Super Bowl XLIII, to coordinate a "look-in" from some of those military members serving abroad. A live satellite feed will show military football fans watching the big game from a military post in the Middle East, he explained.

The NFL wouldn't give specifics on whether the feed would air from Iraq or Afghanistan, but McCarthy said the "look-in" has generally become another staple of Super Bowl broadcasts and tradition, as it's occurred regularly throughout recent years.

"[The NFL] feels that the 70,000 fans attending the Super Bowl this year should be cheering louder for the military than the two teams playing," he said. "It is, indeed, very important for the NFL to look for every opportunity to support the troops."

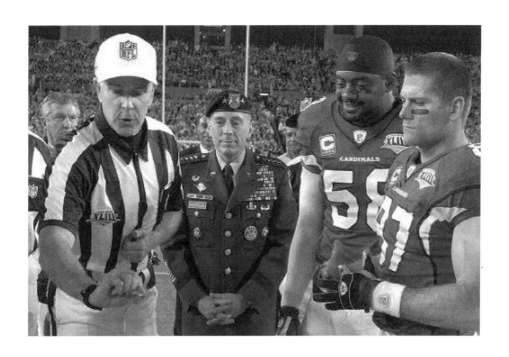

David Petraeus performs the coin toss

NFL Commissioner Roger Goodell, John Elway, and Gen. David Petraeus

David Petraeus and his wife Holly

General Petraeus shakes hands with one of his fans

Pittsburgh Steelers (AFC)

27

Arizona Cardinals (NFC)

23

Gen. David H. Petraeus speaking at the New Hampshire Institute of Politics at Saint Anselm College

On October 31, 2008, Petraeus assumed command of the United States Central Command (USCENTCOM) headquartered in Tampa, Florida. Petraeus was responsible for U.S. operations in 20 countries spreading from Egypt to Pakistan—including Operations Iraqi Freedom and Enduring Freedom. During his time at CENTCOM, Petraeus advocated that countering the terrorist threats in the CENTCOM region requires more than just counter-terrorism forces, demanding instead whole-of-governments, comprehensive approaches akin to those of counterinsurgency. Petraeus reiterated this view in a 2009 interview published in *Parade* magazine. In a recent interview for *Newsweek* magazine's "Interview Issue: The View From People Who Make a Difference", Petraeus expressed his support for President Obama's announced Afghanistan strategy and discussed his view that reconciliation efforts in Afghanistan should for the time being occur "at the lower and midlevels".

In mid-August 2009, Petraeus established the Afghanistan-Pakistan Center of Excellence within the USCENTCOM Directorate of Intelligence to provide leadership to coordinate, integrate and focus analysis efforts in support of operations in Afghanistan and Pakistan.

Afghanistan-Pakistan Center of Excellence

The **Afghanistan-Pakistan Center of Excellence** (AFG-PAK COE) is an internal think tank at the United States Central Command focused on Afghanistan, Pakistan, and the Central Asian States. The AFG-PAK COE seeks to build expertise in and provide improved intelligence for the missions in those countries and the states around them. The AFG-PAK COE is planning to help expand the number of U.S. military and civilian experts on Afghanistan and Pakistan by providing them with education and training opportunities covering the culture, language, and region, and keeping these analysts and military forces connected to these missions in those countries when they are between deployments.

The COE is within the USCENTCOM Directorate of Intelligence.

Petraeus agrees with Obama:
It's time to close Guantanamo and end torture.

May 26, 2009

"*Petraeus agrees with Obama: It's time to close Guantanamo and end torture.*"

In an interview this past weekend with Radio Free Europe, Gen. David Petraeus said that he supports President Obama's decision to close the Guantanamo Bay detention facility and opposes the use of enhanced interrogation techniques:

PETRAEUS: In fact, I have long been on record as having testified and also in helping write doctrine for **interrogation techniques that are completely in line with the Geneva Convention**. And as a division commander in Iraq in the early days, we put out guidance very early on to make sure that our soldiers, in fact, knew that we needed to stay within those guidelines.

With respect to Guantanamo, I think that the closure in a responsible manner, obviously one that is certainly being worked out now by the Department of Justice — I talked to the attorney general the other day [and] they have a very intensive effort ongoing to determine, indeed, what to do with the detainees who are left, how to deal with them in a legal way, and if continued incarceration is necessary — again, how to take that forward.

But doing that in a responsible manner, I think, **sends an important message to the world, as does the commitment of the United States to observe the Geneva Convention when it comes to the treatment of detainees**.

Here are the transcripts from the interview with Radio Free Europe

Transcript: RFE/RL Interviews U.S. Central Command Chief, General David Petraeus

May 24, 2009

General David Petraeus, the commander of U.S. Central Command, sat down with RFE/RL Central Newsroom Director Jay Tolson in Prague on May 24 to talk about a wide range of issues. He answered questions about Guantanamo and "enhanced interrogation techniques," a looming deadline for U.S. troop withdrawal in Iraq, cutting off and combating militant Islamist extremists. Petraeus also talked about successes and setbacks in Afghanistan, Pakistan, and the region, and highlighted the need for international forces to keep Afghan civilian casualties "to an absolute minimum." This is a complete transcript

RFE/RL: Well, thank you for coming here today, General Petraeus, to talk to Radio Free Europe.

Petraeus: Good to be with you, Jay.

**RFE/RL: As you know, General, the debate over Guantanamo and enhanced interrogation techniques has become "Topic A" in Washington. In your view, does the closing of

"Gitmo" and the abandonment of those techniques complicate the U.S. mission in Iraq, Afghanistan, and in the overall struggle against violent transnational extremist groups or does it help it?

Petraeus: I think, on balance, that those moves help it. In fact, I have long been on record as having testified and also in helping write doctrine for interrogation techniques that are completely in line with the Geneva Convention. And as a division commander in Iraq in the early days, we put out guidance very early on to make sure that our soldiers, in fact, knew that we needed to stay within those guidelines.

With respect to Guantanamo, I think that the closure in a responsible manner, obviously one that is certainly being worked out now by the Department of Justice -- I talked to the attorney general the other day [and] they have a very intensive effort ongoing to determine, indeed, what to do with the detainees who are left, how to deal with them in a legal way, and if continued incarceration is necessary -- again, how to take that forward.

But doing that in a responsible manner, I think, sends an important message to the world, as does the commitment of the United States to observe the Geneva Convention when it comes to the treatment of detainees.

RFE/RL: With the approach of the June 20 deadline for the withdrawal of U.S. troops from Iraq's cities, is there a danger that you are removing a key component of the successful security strategy before the Iraq government and military are ready to handle things on their own?

Petraeus: Well, actually, we've been handing over cities and, indeed, entire provinces to the Iraqi security forces for years at this point. The question that revolves around a couple of key cities in which we still have a presence, Baghdad, Mosul, and Baquba to an extent, and ensuring that the Iraqi forces there are certainly ready to ensure the security after the departure of our forces from their streets, which is a process that has already been ongoing.

We believe that the Iraqi forces, indeed, can take this forward. They are in considerably better shape, much more capable and certainly more numerous than they were at the beginning of the surge. There are over 600,000 Iraqi solders, Iraq police, who are helping to take on the security burdens of their country, and we believe that they can do that.

Having said that, there will be periodic attacks, as there have been in the past as Al-Qaeda tries to reignite the sectarian violence that caused such horrific loss of life in the winter of 2006 and into 2007. It is very important to recognize, though, that even as we have seen some of these tragic losses, even just last week, for example, in a so-called sensational attack, a suicide bombing inside Baghdad, that the level of violence remains vastly reduced. It is down from 160 attacks per day, on average, in June of 2007 to between 10 and 15 attacks per day over the last five or six months. And that has remained there despite, again, these occasional "sensational attacks," which do, indeed, cause very tragic loss of life.

Terrorists' Funding

RFE/RL: We know that money from Saudi and various other Gulf states has been the lifeblood of Islamist extremism, including the Taliban. Why, more than eight years after 9/11, have the United States and its allies been unable to cut off this crucial source of funding? Is there anything new that you think should be done?

Petraeus: Well, first of all, I think it is important just to take the Afghan Taliban as an example. There are really three major sources of funding that they receive. There's the money that comes from the illegal narcotics industry, and that is the way to describe it. It is that large, and it is that problematic. There is money that comes from a variety of criminal activities, from kidnapping, from other extortion schemes and essentially mafia-like activity that the Taliban has conducted. And then there is, indeed, still money that comes in from the outside, some perhaps from neighboring countries and some perhaps from the Gulf States.

Saudi Arabia, if asked this question, by the way -- because I have had discussions with Saudi leaders about this, and most recently, the Saudi ambassador in Washington -- I think rightly would say, "You tell me the names of the people and the bank accounts, and we will shut it down." Because they have been, in fact, quite vigilant in shutting down, certainly, state-sponsored provision of money to extremist elements, and when it can be identified, when it can be found, any private activities that are similar to that. But again, these are large countries.

There are staggering amounts of wealth in some of these countries, the Hawala system -- through which much of this is transmitted -- is very difficult to track. It is not computerized, needless to say. It is relatively clandestine in nature. And it is somewhat impervious to the kinds of financial forensics that we can use with transfers that work through actual banking systems.

Threats In Afghanistan And Pakistan

RFE/RL: If the mission in Afghanistan is to ensure that it never again becomes a haven for Al-Qaeda or other violent Islamist groups, does that mean holding the Afghan government to certain nonnegotiable standards of liberal democracy and universal human rights?

Petraeus: Well, certainly there's no question that the Afghan government needs to do a better job in terms of achieving the support of its own people to be seen as legitimate and serving those people. And I think President [Hamid] Karzai would be the first, in fact, to note that and to note that some of the corruption that has been so widely publicized and has caused such problems.

Some of the predatory practices by some elements or individuals of the greater Afghan government indeed need to be curtailed and stopped. It is hugely important that they carry out those actions. There are ambitious anticorruption programs, for example, in the Ministry of Interior launched by Minister [Hanif] Atmar, that are quite impressive. But there obviously needs to be a vast amount more attention given to this if, again, this government is to be seen by the people as serving them and to be worthy of their support.

RFE/RL: To what extent do you think that Pakistan's government and, particularly, its military now understand that Islamist extremism within its borders poses a greater threat than India?

Petraeus: Well, it seems to be to a very increased extent, to a considerable extent. The fact is that the Pakistani military has been moving forces from the Indian [border] with orders to move more having been issued.

The fact is, you have a unique convergence right now of four major elements in Pakistani society: the government, including the major opposition figures, Nawaz Sharif and others. Virtually all the political parties, with a couple of exceptions, are united in saying that Pakistan must oppose and confront the Taliban and the other extremists in their country who do, indeed, threaten the very existence of the Pakistani state.

In addition to that, the people now, really for the first time, very much oppose what the Taliban has shown itself to do. There was some hope, I think, at one time, that perhaps the Taliban could provide something that the government was not providing: speedy justice, swift justice, as they say, in the Northwest Frontier Province. That now has been shown to be a myth and, in fact, the oppressive practices that the Taliban brought into Swat and then into Buner and Lower Dir, for example, showed what the rest of Pakistan would have if, in fact, the Taliban was allowed to expand its oppressive practices further. You also have, uniquely, [the fact that] the religious leaders have issued fatwas against the Taliban.

And with all of this, certainly the Pakistani military is very aggressively prosecuting the campaign in the Northwest Frontier Province and also continuing its activities in the Federally Administered Tribal Areas. I think that this is unique, since 9/11 certainly, and it bodes much better for Pakistan and for the hope of Pakistan as a country that is, compared to the Taliban, a moderate country that is tolerant and not one in which religious, ultraconservative, or extremist figures can tell the people how to pray, how to groom themselves, what music they can listen to, and all the rest of that.

Afghan Civilian Casualties

RFE/RL: While the counterinsurgency strategy you advocate concentrates on winning hearts and minds, the "human terrain" as the U.S. military now calls it, coalition air strikes against insurgents in Afghanistan appear to be having exactly the opposite effect. Do you see this problem being resolved anytime soon?

Petraeus: Well, first of all, it is a problem, and it is one that we must address and we must continue to work at how we can ensure that we still have access to these very important enablers, as we call them.

We shouldn't have our soldiers go into a fight with one arm tied behind their back. On the other hand, we have to figure out how to bring these forces, these combat elements to bear without, obviously, killing innocent civilians.

And it is very, very difficult in some cases because the Taliban has been shown to use civilians almost as human shields or at least to provoke firing into areas where there are civilians.

There is a tactical directive that was issued General [David] McKiernan, the ISAF [International Security Assistance Force] commander. The application of that and also a number of other techniques that have been employed to partner Afghan and our special-operations forces in various techniques has seemed to work.

But still, there are cases, such as the one, certainly, in western Afghanistan several weeks ago in which innocent civilians were killed in significant numbers. And we won't debate the numbers. What we need to do is figure out how to move forward and how to avoid such cases and to keep them to an absolute minimum in the future.

So there is an investigation that I directed, [with a] brigadier general brought in from the United States with considerable time on the ground in Afghanistan and in Iraq, both as a special operator and as a conventional-forces deputy commander. And he is looking at this with a team. I will meet with them in Kabul...[to] review the initial findings as they finalize their investigation, and then see what that says about the need to either modify the directive, to suggest that to the NATO authorities, or, at the very least, to ensure the very proper training and education of our forces on the application of that directive.

RFE/RL: The Taliban and other Afghan insurgent groups are insisting on a U.S. pullout as a condition for peace talks, while your idea of reconciliation is a bottom-up, localized approach, of peeling away the foot soldiers from the hard-line core. How do you see reconciliation actually moving forward in Afghanistan?

Petraeus: Well, I think it is, most probably, to be more of a bottom-up approach. I think that negotiating with individuals who think that they are in the ascendant, who have some degree of momentum, at least in their own minds, certainly have increased the level of violence in Afghanistan significantly in the past two years, whose criteria is to remove those who are most helping the Afghan government, obviously doesn't hold much promise for improved security or progress for the Afghan people.

So, most likely, it is to be local elements to help re-empower, reestablish the traditional social structures, the mullah, the Malik, the tribal elders, the religious leaders at local levels who traditionally have always ensured the resolution of disputes at local levels, who have looked after the people of their tribes and so forth, while helping to extend the national government so that the two of those can connect in a productive and constructive manner. I think that is more likely to be the road ahead.

But clearly what you want to do is to determine who are the reconcilables, who are the irreconcilables. And you should not shrink from the fact that the irreconcilables have to be killed, captured, or run out of the country.

Central Asian Equation

RFE/RL: The Central Asian states all agree that the region's biggest security problems right now emanate from Afghanistan. Given that, why, in your opinion, has it been so difficult for some of them to commit more firmly to helping the U.S. and NATO efforts?

Petraeus: Well, I think if I could discuss what, perhaps, might be most beneficial for the Central Asian states and really all of the countries -- including my own and Russia and the other great powers of the world -- indeed would be to recognize that the common threats to the Central Asian states. And those are extremism coming out of Afghanistan, Pakistan, from the south, if you will, and the illegal narcotics industry that has enslaved so many people in the Central Asian states, even in Iran by the way, and works its way up into Russia as well.

These common threats warrant cooperation and a broad partnership rather than continued zero sum approaches to the new "Great Game," if you will, the competition for power and resources in the Central Asian states.

The fact is, actually, that I've visited every one of these states, their leaders, in the past four months or so, and we have, in fact, achieved agreements with them and even Russia now is supportive of the movement of cargo, supplies, and so forth through their borders. [There are] different arrangements with different countries -- a very important agreement with Uzbekistan, in particular, because all roads do lead through Uzbekistan and into Afghanistan. But we do see this kind of partnership that has developed, to a degree, and is one on which we hope we can build in the future.

On March 16, 2010, testimony to the Senate Armed Services Committee, Petraeus described the continuing Israeli–Palestinian conflict as a challenge to U.S. interests in the region. According to the testimony, the conflict was "fomenting anti-American sentiment" due to "a perception of U.S. favoritism for Israel". This was widely commented on in the media. When questioned by journalist Philip Klein, Petraeus said the original reporter "picked apart" and "spun" his speech. He believes there are many important factors standing in the way of peace, including "a whole bunch of extremist organizations, some of which by the way deny Israel's right to exist. There's a country that has a nuclear program who denies that the Holocaust took place. So again we have all these factors in there. This [Israel] is just one."

In March 2010, Petraeus visited the New Hampshire Institute of Politics at Saint Anselm College to speak about Iraq and Afghanistan. Petraeus spoke a few days after the seventh anniversary of the U.S. invasion of Iraq, noting the successful changes in Iraq since the U.S. troop surge. The visit to Saint Anselm created rumors that Petraeus was contemplating a run for the Presidency; however, he denied the speculation saying that he was not aware that the college has been the site of numerous presidential debates.

Toward the close of his tenure as CENTCOM Commander, including in his interview published in *Vanity Fair*, Petraeus discussed the effort to determine and send to Afghanistan the right "inputs" for success there; these inputs include several structures and organizations that proved important in Iraq, including "an engagement cell to support reconciliation...a finance cell to go after financing of the enemy...[a] really robust detainee-operations task force, a rule-of-law task force, an energy-fusion cell – all these other sort of nonstandard missions that are very important."

On May 5, 2010, the New York Times published an article that there was mounting evidence of a Taliban role in the Times Square bombing plot. On May 7, 2010, Petraeus announced that Times Square bombing suspect, Faisal Shahzad, is a "lone wolf" terrorist who did not work with others. On May 10, 2010, Attorney General Eric Holder said that the evidence shows the Pakistani Taliban directed this plot.

Mug shot of Faisal Shahzad

Commander of U.S. and ISAF forces in Afghanistan

Petraeus having tea with the Afghan Border Police Commander at the border with Uzbekistan

On June 23, 2010, President Obama announced that he would nominate Petraeus to succeed General Stanley A. McChrystal as the commander of U.S. Forces in Afghanistan. The change of command was prompted by McChrystal's comments about the Obama administration and its policies in Afghanistan during an interview with *Rolling Stone* magazine. The nomination was technically a positional step down from his position as commander of Central Command, however the President said that he believed that he was the best man for the job. After being confirmed by the Senate on June 30, Petraeus formally assumed command on July 4. During the assumption of command remarks, Petraeus provided his vision and goals to NATO, the members of his command, and his Afghan partners. As he was known to do while the Commander in Iraq, Petraeus delivered his first Letter to the Troops on the same day he assumed command.

On August 1, 2010, shortly after the disclosure of the Afghan war logs on Wikileaks, Petraeus issued his updated Tactical Directive for the prevention of civilian casualties, providing guidance and intent for the use of force by the U.S. military units operating in Afghanistan (replacing the July 1, 2009 version). This directive reinforced the concept of "disciplined use of force in partnership with Afghan Security Forces" in the fight against insurgent forces.

We must never forget that the center of gravity in this struggle is the Afghan people; it is they who will ultimately determine the future of Afghanistan ... Prior to the use of fires, the commander approving the strike must determine that no civilians are present. If unable to assess the risk of civilian presence, fires are prohibited, except under of the following two conditions (specific conditions deleted due to operational security; however, they have to do with the risk to ISAF and Afghan forces).

In the October 2010 issue of *Army Magazine*, Petraeus discussed changes that had taken place over the previous 18 months, including sections discussing "setting the conditions for progress", "capitalizing on the conditions for progress", "improving security", "supporting governance expansion", "promoting economic development", "reducing corruption", and "our troopers: carrying out a difficult mission".

Former 101st general replacing ousted U.S. commander in Afghanistan

Newspaper report June 23, 2010

Maj. Gen. David H. Petraeus, then-commander of the 101st Airborne Division (Air Assault) and Fort Campbell, kisses his daughter, Anne, while hugging his wife, Holly, upon his return from Operation Iraqi Freedom in 2004 at Campbell Army Air Field.

WASHINGTON (AP) — President Barack Obama ousted Gen. Stanley McChrystal as the top U.S. commander in Afghanistan on Wednesday, choosing the embattled general's direct boss — Gen. David Petraeus — to take over the troubled 9-year-old war, a source told The Associated Press.

Petraeus is the former commander of Fort Campbell and the 101st Airborne Division (Air Assault).

McChrystal was summoned to Washington from Kabul to explain scathing, mocking remarks about administration officials, including Obama and Vice President Joe Biden, by him and his team in a magazine article. But the morning showdown with Obama in the Oval Office was not enough to save his job.

McChrystal offered his resignation and Obama accepted it, said the source, who spoke on condition of anonymity because the president's decision was not yet made public.

Obama planned to speak at 1:30 p.m. EDT from the Rose Garden, accompanied by Defense Secretary Robert Gates and Adm. Mike Mullen, chairman of the Joint Chiefs of Staff, about the controversy.

Petraeus, who attended a formal Afghanistan war meeting at the White House Wednesday, now oversees the wars in both Afghanistan and Iraq as head of U.S. Central Command.

By pairing the decision on McChrystal's departure with the name of his replacement, Obama is seeking to move on as quickly as possible from the firestorm surrounding the Rolling Stone magazine story and the renewed debate over his Afghanistan policy that it provoked.

With Washington abuzz about this controversy, there was an almost complete lockdown on information about the morning's developments. It was not even known where McChrystal went after his half-hour meeting with Obama at the White House, which came not long after his early morning arrival from Afghanistan.

Petraeus is the nation's best-known military man, having risen to prominence as the commander who turned around the Iraq war in 2007. The Afghanistan job is actually a step down from his current post.

Petraeus has a reputation for rigorous discipline and careful attention to his image. He keeps a punishing pace — spending more than 300 days on the road last year.

Petraeus briefly collapsed during Senate testimony last week, apparently from dehydration. It was a rare glimpse of weakness for a man known as among the military's most driven.

He is also among the brightest, and rose to command through a mix of brains and now has been adapted for Afghanistan.

Petraeus has repeatedly denied that he plans to run for president in 2012, and is said to want only one job: chairman of the Joint Chiefs of Staff.

In the hearing last week, Petraeus told Congress he would recommend delaying the pullout of U.S. forces from Afghanistan beginning in July 2011 if need be, saying security and political conditions in Afghanistan must be ready to handle a U.S. drawdown.

That does not mean Petraeus is opposed to bringing some troops home, and he said repeatedly that he supports the new Afghanistan strategy that Obama announced in December. Petraeus' caution is rooted in the fact that the uniformed military — and counterinsurgency specialists in particular — have always been uncomfortable with fixed parameters.

Petraeus gives Obama 'manly man' shirt

12/3/2010

Before speaking to troops in Afghanistan, President Obama got a present from Gen. David Petraeus -- a "manly man T-shirt." The reason? So no one ever elbows Obama in the face during a basketball game again.

Not one but two shirts were considered, after the first -- a standard-issue shirt from the International Security Assistance, the formal name of the NATO-led mission in Afghanistan -- was deemed insufficiently big and bad. Obama was given a 101st Airborne T-shirt instead. "No one will mess with you if you wear this, Mr. President," Petraeus declared.

GEN. PETRAEUS: Good evening to you all! How about a "HOO-ah"!

SOLDIERS: HOOO-AHHHHH!

GEN. PETRAEUS: How about an "Air Assault"!

SOLDIERS: Air Assault!

GEN. PETRAEUS: Ah, we gotta try that again. How about an "Air Assault"!

SOLDIERS: AIR ASSAULT!

GEN. PETRAEUS: Anybody out -- (audio break) -- everybody ready for the main event? (Cheers.) You sure about that? (Cheers.)

Okay. Here's the deal. Couple of years ago, my air assault buddy at the time -- at the time, command sergeant major of the 101st Airborne Division -- (cheers) -- Command Sergeant Major Marvin Hill, told me what he looks for in a commander. He listed all of the usual qualities that you'd expect -- you know all the ones -- and then he added: I also want a commander who is available to our troopers, who is accessible to our troopers and who is approachable.

Now, as I thought about it, I realized that in addition to all the qualities we expect in leaders, I also look for those specific attributes. And this evening, it is my honor to introduce to you a leader who has demonstrated his concern for each of you; who's already been to the hospital to pin Purple Hearts on some of our wounded warriors, to meet with a platoon that suffered tragic loss; and who has proven above all that he is available, accessible and approachable, by flying halfway around the world to be here with us tonight.

Fellow warriors, please join me in welcoming the leader who made the tough decision to provide us the resources that have enabled progress here in Afghanistan, the president of the United States of America, our commander in chief, President Barack Obama. (Cheers, applause.)

Okay. But before the president starts, I think you all know the president was out on the basketball court a few days ago. Now he'd beaten that team four times already. He'd just scored on the guy, and elbows started flying around. Now the only explanation we can come up with is that they forgot who they were playing with. And so Sergeant Major Hill, still my air assault buddy, decided we'd give him a T- shirt.

Well, okay. I got it. It's not the biggest, baddest. It's an ISAF T-shirt. It's hoo-ah. But then -- (cheers) -- yeah, okay. But then the commander, the 43rd commander of the 101st Airborne Division -- (cheers) -- came up with a manly man T-shirt, and no one will mess with you if you wear this, Mr. President.

Huh! (Cheers, applause.)

PRESIDENT OBAMA: I'm sorry, Bagram. I can't hear you. (Cheers, applause.) Air assault!

Petraeus visits Regional Command West in Afghanistan, May 16, 2011

In early March 2011, Petraeus made a "rare apology" following a NATO helicopter airstrike under his command which resulted in the deaths of nine Afghan boys and the wounding of a 10th, as they gathered firewood in Eastern Afghanistan. In a statement, Petraeus apologized to the members of the Afghan government, the people of Afghanistan and the surviving family members, and said: "These deaths should have never happened." Several journalists and observers noted the humanitarian candor in Petraeus' open regrets. Petraeus relinquished command of U.S. and NATO forces in Afghanistan on July 18. He received the Defense Distinguished Service Medal and the NATO Meritorious Service Medal for his service.

Joint Task Force-101 Transfer of Authority Ceremony

May 19, 2011

Transfer of Authority from CJTF-101 to CJTF-1 – 101st Airborne Division Colors Cased

Bagram Airfield, Afghanistan – On May 19th, 2011 the Transfer of Authority Ceremony from combined Joint Task Force-101 to Combined Joint Task Force-1 took place at Bagram Airfield, Afghanistan.

General David H. Petraeus, Commander, U.S. Forces Afghanistan, was on hand for the ceremony and spoke with (outgoing) Major General John F. Campbell, Commander, Regional Command – East, as well as (incoming) Major General Daniel B. Allyn, Commander, Regional Command – East.

(Left to right) General David H. Petraeus, Commander, U.S. Forces-Afghanistan, (outgoing) Maj. Gen. John F. Campbell, Commander, Regional Command – East, Lt. Gen. David M. Rodriguez, Commander, International Security Assistance Force joint Command and Deputy Commander, U.S. Forces-Afghanistan, and (incoming) Maj. Gen. Daniel B. Allyn, Commander, Regional Command – East, line up before marching to the Combined Joint Task Force-101 to Combined Joint Task Force-1 Transfer of Authority ceremony.

During the Combined Joint Task Force-101 to Combined Joint Task Force-1 Transfer of Authority ceremony, Maj. Gen. John F. Campbell and Command Sergeant Major Scott C. Schroeder cased the colors of the 101st Airborne Division (Air Assault) for the return Fort Campbell, KY.

Major General John F. Campbell and Command Sgt. Maj. Scott C. Schroeder, commander and command sergeant major of the 101st Airborne Division (Air Assault), will be welcomed home to Fort Campbell, KY, May 20th at 8:00 a.m..

Photo Gallery

Petraeus recognizes TF Currahee soldiers for combat actions

Jul 9, 2011

PAKTIKA PROVINCE, Afghanistan - U.S. Army Gen. David H. Petraeus, commander of International Security Assistance Force and commander of U.S. Forces-Afghanistan visited soldiers with Task Force Currahee, 4th Brigade Combat Team, 101st Airborne Division, at Forward Operating Base Sharana July 7, to present awards as part of his final farewell tour before transitioning to CIA director.

Petraeus holds significant ties to TF Currahee. He was the 101st Airborne Division commander when discussions to reactivate the regiment began and he played a key role in planning their 2005 reactivation.

"As I was coming out here, I realized this was probably my last battlefield circulation," said Petraeus. "What better unit, in truth, to be visiting for what is an emotional event, in a lot of ways."

"I want you, above all, to have pride, quiet pride, in what it is that you have achieved," he said. "This is a truly historic regiment. I don't need to tell you that. A lot of us back in the day were lobbying to get this regiment brought back on active duty, and I can tell you that the decision was made when I was Eagle 6."

The ISAF commander had words of praise for the Currahees and their efforts throughout Paktika province.

"You all have done a magnificent job over the course of the last year [against] very difficult terrain and a very difficult enemy right up against the border," he said. "You have truly distinguished yourself in that fight, you've made inroads, especially as you come to the end of your tour."

"Most importantly, we're very, very proud to see the new chapters that you all have written for the history of this extraordinary regiment," said Petraeus.

As his remarks came to a close, Petraeus spoke of what it means to a commander to be able to recognize Soldiers who have displayed bravery in battle.

"What an honor, to be able to recognize a few of our heroes here today with Purple Hearts, awards for valor and Combat Action Badges," he said. "There's no greater privilege for a commander than to recognize those who have done something exceptional and again, I feel very privileged to be able to do that here with you today."

Petraeus was not the only one who felt privileged; the soldiers receiving awards from the commander said they were awestruck by the experience.

U.S. Army Pfc. James R. Morrison, an infantryman with "Dog" Company, 2nd Battalion, 506th Infantry Regiment, 4th BCT, 101st Airborne Div. and native of Rockland County, N.Y., ran through enemy fire to reach a weapon that was used to push the enemy back. He was awarded an Army Commendation Medal with Valor device, but was left without words as he was recognized by the outgoing commander.

"I was speechless," said Morrison. "It would have been an honor to be recognized by the brigade commander, but Gen. Petraeus is the commander of all of Afghanistan; this is something I never expected to happen in my lifetime."

U.S. Army Pfc. Christopher W. Mioduszewski, also an infantryman with "Dog" Company, 2nd Bn., 506th Inf. Regt., 4th BCT, 101st Airborne Div., and native of Erie, Pa., was in the same fire fight as Morrison and was the first line of defense against the enemy.

"I was the front-line gun during initial contact," said Mioduszewski. "I was one of the main heavy weapons that was firing to push the enemy back."

Alone in his position, he held his ground against the enemy. He had mixed feelings about being awarded the ARCOM with Valor device from Petraeus.

"Getting the award from him was pretty sweet," said Mioduszewski. "It would have been better to have the guys that were there with me that day, but it really felt good to be recognized."

Both soldiers said they were humbled by the experience and had thoughts of their teammates as they were awarded.

"If it wasn't for my team, I know I would have never been able to make it to the other position, so this is definitely for them too," said Morrison.

As he was preparing to depart, Petraeus asked each of the soldiers to pause and to "think about what you have accomplished and take pride in it."

U.S. Army Gen. David H. Petraeus, commander of International Security Assistance Force and commander of U.S. Forces Afghanistan talks with Task Force Currahee soldiers from 4th Brigade Combat Team, 101st Airborne Division July 7, at Forward Operating Base Sharana in Afghanistan's Paktika Province.

U.S. Army Gen. David H. Petraeus, commander of International Security Assistance Force and commander of U.S. Forces Afghanistan, pauses for a photo after pinning the Army Commendation Medal with Valor device on U.S. Army Pfc. James R. Morrison, an infantryman with "Dog" Company, 2nd Battalion, 506th Infantry Regiment, 4th Brigade Combat Team, 101st Airborne Division and native of Rockland County, N.Y., July 7, at Forward Operating Base Sharana in Afghanistan's Paktika province.

U.S. Army Gen. David H. Petraeus, commander of International Security Assistance Force and commander of U.S. Forces Afghanistan pins the Army Commendation Medal with Valor device on U.S. Army Pfc. Christopher W. Mioduszewski, an infantryman with "Dog" Company, 2nd Battalion, 506th Infantry Regiment, 4th Brigade Combat Team, 101st Airborne Division and native of Erie, Pa., July 7, at Forward Operating Base Sharana.

Task Force Currahee soldiers from 4th Brigade Combat Team, 101st Airborne Division after being recognized for their valorous actions in combat by U.S. Army Gen. David H. Petraeus, commander of International Security Assistance Force and commander of U.S. Forces Afghanistan, pause for a group photo July 7, at Forward Operating Base Sharana.

U.S. Army Gen. David H. Petraeus, commander of International Security Assistance Force and commander of U.S. Forces Afghanistan talks with Task Force Currahee soldiers from 4th Brigade Combat Team, 101st Airborne Division July 7, at Forward Operating Base Sharana in Afghanistan's Paktika province.

Over the 36 years that David Petraeus served our country he advanced from a second lieutenant in 1974 to a 4 star General in 2007. Here are the dates of rank.

Promotions

Rank	Date
Second Lieutenant	1974
First Lieutenant	1976
Captain	1978
Major	1985
Lieutenant Colonel	1991
Colonel	1995
Brigadier General	2000
Major General	2003
Lieutenant General	2004
General	2007

Retirement from the U.S. Army

Petraeus retired from the U.S. Army on August 31, 2011. His retirement ceremony was held at Joint Base Myer-Henderson Hall. During this ceremony, he was awarded the Army Distinguished Service Medal by Deputy Secretary of Defense William J. Lynn.

General David Petraeus awarded the Army Distinguished Service Medal

by Deputy Secretary of Defense William J. Lynn

During the ceremony, Lynn in his remarks noted that, General Petraeus has played an important role as both a combat leader and strategist in the post-9/11 world. Lynn also cited General Petraeus' efforts in current counter insurgency strategy. Admiral Michael Mullen, Chairman of the Joint Chiefs of Staff in his remarks compared General Petraeus to Ulysses S. Grant, John J. Pershing, George Marshall and Dwight D. Eisenhower as one of the great battle captains of American history. For his 38 years of service Petraeus receives a $220,000 annual pension.

CIA Director

Petraeus ceremonially sworn in at CIA Headquarters as his wife, Holly, looks on

On April 28, 2011, President Barack Obama announced that he had nominated Petraeus to become the new Director of the Central Intelligence Agency. The nomination was confirmed by the United States Senate 94–0 on June 30, 2011. Petraeus was sworn in at the White House on September 6 and then ceremonially sworn in by Vice President Joe Biden at CIA Headquarters in Langley, Virginia on October 11, 2011.

Petraeus' tenure at the CIA was more low profile than that of his predecessor, Leon Panetta, declining to give media interviews while Director and speaking to Congress in closed sessions. He also differed from Panetta in management style, as an article in *The New York Times* published just days before his resignation said Panetta "wooed the work force and often did not question operational details, [while] Petraeus is a demanding boss who does not hesitate to order substandard work redone or details of plans adjusted."

Although Petraeus was given good marks by most observers for his work heading the CIA, during October 2012 some critics took issue with the availability of accurate information from the CIA concerning a terrorist attack in Benghazi, Libya, the month prior. On September 11 four Americans had been killed, including the Ambassador, and more than thirty evacuated. Only seven of those evacuated did not work for the CIA. According to a Wall Street Journal story, other government agencies complained about being left "largely in the dark about the CIA's role," with Secretary of State Hillary Clinton telephoning Petraeus directly the night of the attacks seeking assistance. Although the "State Department believed it had a formal agreement with the CIA to provide backup security," "the CIA didn't have the same understanding about its security responsibilities," said the Wall Street Journal.

The Benghazi Incident

Nov. 16: Ex CIA Director David Petraeus Testifies before Congress

Petraeus: CIA blamed terrorists for Libya Attack

Testifying out of sight, ex-CIA Director David Petraeus told Congress Friday that classified intelligence showed the deadly raid on the U.S. Consulate in Libya was a terrorist attack but the administration withheld the suspected role of al-Qaida affiliates to avoid tipping them off.

The recently resigned spy chief explained that references to terrorist groups suspected of carrying out the violence were removed from the public explanation of what caused the attack so as not to alert them that U.S. intelligence was on their trail, according to lawmakers who attended Petraeus' private briefings.

He also said it initially was unclear whether the militants had infiltrated a demonstration to cover their attack.

The retired four-star general addressed the House and Senate intelligence committees in back-to-back, closed-door hearings as questions persist over what the Obama administration knew in the immediate aftermath of the Sept. 11 attacks and why its public description did not match intelligence agencies' assessments.

After the hearings, lawmakers who questioned Petraeus said he testified that the CIA's draft talking points in response to the assault on the diplomatic post in Benghazi that killed four Americans referred to it as a terrorist attack. Petraeus said that reference was removed from the final version, although he wasn't sure which federal agency deleted it.

Adding to the explanation, a senior U.S. official familiar with the drafting of the points said later that a reason the references to al-Qaida were deleted was that the information came from classified sources and the links were, and still are, tenuous. The administration also did not want to prejudice a criminal investigation in its early stages, that official said, speaking on condition of anonymity because the official was not authorized to discuss the process publicly.

Senate Intelligence Committee Chair Sen. Dianne Feinstein, D-Calif. is surrounded by reporters after …

Democrats said Petraeus made it clear the change was not done for political reasons during President Barack Obama's re-election campaign.

"The general was adamant there was no politicization of the process, no White House interference or political agenda," said Rep. Adam Schiff, D-Calif. "He completely debunked that idea."

But Republicans remain critical of the administration's handling of the case. Sen. Marco Rubio, R-Fla., said Petraeus' testimony showed that "clearly the security measures were inadequate despite an overwhelming and growing amount of information that showed the area in Benghazi was dangerous, particularly on the night of Sept. 11."

In fact, Petraeus told lawmakers that protesters literally walked in and set fire to the facility, according to a congressional official who attended the briefing. U.S. Ambassador Chris Stevens died from smoke inhalation. Petraeus said security at the CIA annex was much better, but the attackers had armaments to get in.

Separately on Friday, the Democratic leader in the Senate rejected a request from John McCain and two other senators for a Watergate-style congressional committee to investigate the

Benghazi attack. In a letter to McCain, Sen. Harry Reid said several committees in the House and Senate are already investigating and he would not allow the Senate to be used as a "venue for baseless partisan attacks." Republican House Speaker John Boehner also said this week that a special committee was not necessary.

Senate Intelligence Committee member Sen. Bill Nelson, D-Fla., speaks with reporters on Capitol Hill …

Petraeus, who had a long and distinguished military career, was giving his first Capitol Hill testimony since resigning last week in disgrace over an extramarital affair with his biographer, Paula Broadwell. Lawmakers said he did not discuss that scandal except to express regret about the circumstances of his departure and say that Benghazi had nothing to do with his decision to resign.

He was brought to a secure room beneath the Capitol, avoiding crowds of photographers and television cameras.

Petraeus testified that the CIA draft written in response to the raid referred to militant groups Ansar al-Shariah and al-Qaida in the Islamic Maghreb but that those names were replaced with the word "extremist" in the final draft, according to a congressional staff member. The staffer said Petraeus testified that he allowed other agencies to alter the talking points as they saw fit without asking for final review, to get them out quickly.

The congressional officials weren't authorized to discuss the hearing publicly and described Petraeus' testimony to The Associated Press on condition of anonymity.

Sen. Mark Udall, D-Colo., said Petraeus explained that the CIA's draft points were sent to other intelligence agencies and to some federal agencies for review. Udall said Petraeus told them the final document was put in front of all the senior agency leaders, including him, and everyone signed off on it.

"The assessment that was publicly shared in unclassified talking points went through a process of editing," Udall said. "The extremist description was put in because in an unclassified document you want to be careful who you identify as being involved."

Rep. Peter King, R-N.Y., said it remained unclear how the final talking points developed. The edited version was used by U.N. Ambassador Susan Rice five days after the attack when the White House sent her out for a series of television interviews. Republicans have criticized Rice for saying it appeared the attack was sparked by a spontaneous protest over an anti-Muslim video.

"The fact is, the reference to al-Qaida was taken out somewhere along the line by someone outside the intelligence community," King said. "We need to find out who did it and why."

King said Petraeus had briefed the House committee on Sept. 14, and he did not recall Petraeus being so positive at that time that it was a terrorist attack. "He thought all along that he made it clear there was terrorist involvement," King said. "That was not my recollection."

After two hours with Petraeus, the Democratic chairman of the Senate's intelligence committee and the panel's top Republican sparred over Rice's televised comments.

Chairman Dianne Feinstein of California said Rice relied on "unclassified talking points at a very early stage. ... I don't think she should have been pilloried for this."

Feinstein recalled the faulty intelligence of the George W. Bush administration, used to justify the invasion of Iraq in concluding that country had weapons of mass destruction.

"A lot of people were killed based on bad intelligence," she said. Feinstein added that mistakes were made in the initial intelligence on Benghazi, but she said, "I don't think that's fair game" to blame Rice — who has been mentioned as a possible nominee for secretary of state. "To say she is unqualified to be secretary of state I think is a mistake."

Top committee Republican Sen. Saxby Chambliss of Georgia said Rice had gone beyond the talking points.

"She even mentioned that under the leadership of Barack Obama we had decimated al-Qaida. She knew at that point in time that al-Qaida was responsible in part or in whole for the death of Ambassador Stevens," Chambliss said.

Schiff, the California congressman, said Petraeus had said Rice's comments in the television interviews "reflected the best intelligence at the time that could be released publicly."

"There was an interagency process to draft it, not a political process," Schiff said. "They came up with the best assessment without compromising classified information or source or methods. So changes were made to protect classified information."

Sen. Kent Conrad, D-N.D., said it's clear that Rice "used the unclassified talking points that the entire intelligence community signed off on, so she did completely the appropriate thing." He said the changes made to the draft account for the discrepancies with some of the reports that were made public showing that the intelligence community knew it was a terrorist attack all along.

Lawmakers spent hours Thursday interviewing top intelligence and national security officials, trying to determine what intelligence agencies knew before, during and after the attack. They were shown a video to illustrate the chronology of the attack, which edited together security video from the consulate and surveillance footage taken by an unarmed CIA Predator drone, and even local Libyan cellphone footage taken from YouTube showing Stevens being carried out by people who looked like they were trying to rescue him.

A U.S. official who viewed it said the video shows clearly there was no demonstration prior to the attack, and then, suddenly armed men started streaming into the mission. The official spoke on condition of anonymity because the official was not authorized to discuss the investigation publicly.

Ex-CIA chief Petraeus testifies Benghazi attack was al Qaeda-linked terrorism

Petraeus hearing doesn't clear confusion

Washington -- Former CIA Director David Petraeus testified on Capitol Hill Friday that the attack on the U.S. Consulate in Benghazi, Libya, in September was an act of terrorism committed by al Qaeda-linked militants.

That's according to U.S. Rep. Peter King, R-New York, who spoke to reporters after a closed hearing in the House, which lasted an hour and 20 minutes.

King said Petraeus' testimony differed from an earlier assessment the former CIA director gave lawmakers just days after the September 11 attack, which left four Americans dead, including U.S. Ambassador Chris Stevens.

"He (Petraeus) ... stated that he thought all along he made it clear that there was significant terrorist involvement, and that is not my recollection of what he told us on September 14," King

"The clear impression we were given (in September) was that the overwhelming amount of evidence was that it arose out of a spontaneous demonstration, and was not a terrorist attack," he said.

U.S. officials initially said the violence erupted spontaneously amid a large protest about a privately made video produced in the United States that mocked the Prophet Mohammed.

The intelligence community later revised its assessment, saying it believes the attack was a planned terrorist assault.

King said that the word spontaneous was minimized during Petraeus' testimony Friday, which was given one week after he resigned from the CIA. Lawmakers said they didn't ask him about why he left the agency. Petraeus has admitted an extramarital affair with his biographer.

Critics of the administration have suggested that his resignation might be linked to fallout over the attack.

The Benghazi attack became a political hot button during a presidential election year and raised questions regarding issues such as security at the compound and the Obama administration's initial description of the events.

King told reporters that he likes Petraeus and that it was uncomfortable, at times, to interview a man he considers a friend.

"He was a strong soldier. Very professional, very knowledgeable, very strong," King said. "He's a solid guy. I consider him a friend, which made the questioning tough. You realize the human tragedy here."

After he spoke at the House Intelligence hearing, Petraeus testified in front of the Senate Intelligence Committee. He was ushered into both sessions without reporters being able to get a camera shot of him, and after he testified he left the premises, CNN learned.

Petraeus was not asked to testify under oath, King said.

King and other lawmakers said Petraeus testified that his resignation had nothing to do with the consulate attack.

That matches what Petraeus told Kyra Phillips of HLN, CNN's sister network. He said his resignation was solely a result of his extramarital affair with his biographer, Paula Broadwell. He added that he never passed classified information to her.

Prior to Friday's hearings, it was thought that Petraeus would tell lawmakers that the CIA knew soon after the attack that Ansar al Sharia was responsible for it, according to an official with knowledge of the case. The official spoke on condition of anonymity because of the sensitivity of the subject matter.

Ansar al Sharia is more of a label than an organization, one that's been adopted by conservative Salafist groups across the Arab world.

It was not known whether Petraeus spoke specifically about Ansar al Sharia during Friday's sessions.

After the House committee hearing, Rep. Dutch Ruppersberger, D-Maryland, said the confusion over the consulate incident arose from there being essentially two threads of violence: one caused by the protest, which was chaotic, and a second that was orchestrated by terrorists, which was highly coordinated.

There were "two different types of situations at play," Ruppersberger said, explaining that in the hours and days after the attack, it was naturally difficult to clearly discern what happened.

Intelligence evolves, he said, and new information comes out when agents obtain it. He played down the idea that there was something untoward going on.

The former CIA chief has said there was a stream of intelligence from multiple sources, including video at the scene, that indicated Ansar al Sharia was behind the attack, according to an official with knowledge of the situation.

Meanwhile, separate intelligence indicated the violence at the consulate was inspired by protests in Egypt over an ostensibly anti-Islam film clip that was privately produced in the United States. The movie, "Innocence of Muslims," portrayed the Prophet Mohammed as a womanizing buffoon.

There were 20 intelligence reports that indicated that anger about the film may be to blame, the official said.

The CIA eventually disproved those reports, but not before Petraeus' initial briefing to Congress when he discussed who might be behind the attack and what prompted it. During that briefing, he raised Ansar al Sharia's possible connection as well as outrage about the film, the official said.

Earlier, an official said that Petraeus' aim in testifying was to clear up "a lot of misrepresentations of what he told Congress initially."

Petraeus testified that he developed unclassified talking points in the days after the attack but he had no direct involvement in developing the ones used by Susan Rice, the U.S. ambassador to the United Nations, King said.

"No one knows, yet, exactly who came up with the final version of the talking points, other than to say the original talking points prepared by the CIA were different from the ones that were finally put out," said King, stressing that the original talking points were more specific about al Qaeda involvement.

Rice has been under fire for suggesting the attack on the consulate was a spontaneous event spurred by a protest against the anti-Muslim film.

The three unclassified talking points that were used by Rice on September 16 were read aloud to reporters on the Hill Friday.

They are:

-- The currently available information suggests that the demonstrations in Benghazi were spontaneously inspired by the protests at the US Embassy in Cairo and evolved into a direct assault against the U.S. diplomatic post in Benghazi and subsequently its annex. There are indications that extremists participated in the violent demonstrations.

-- This assessment may change as additional information is collected and analyzed and as currently available information continues to be evaluated.

-- The investigation is ongoing, and the U.S. government is working with Libyan authorities to bring to justice those responsible for the deaths of U.S. citizens.

Sen. Dianne Feinstein, the California Democrat who leads the Intelligence Committee, read the points to journalists and vigorously defended Rice.

Feinstein said lawmakers should be careful not to "pillory" someone for intelligence failings.

"We have seen wrong intelligence before and it all surrounded our going into Iraq, and a lot of people were killed based on bad intelligence," she said. "And I don't think that is fair game. I think mistakes get made. You don't pillory the person.

"To select Ambassador Rice because she used an unclassified talking point, to say that she is unqualified to be secretary of state, I think, is a mistake," the senior lawmaker said. "And the way it keeps going it is almost as if the intent is to assassinate her character."

There has been speculation that Rice was among the people being considered as a replacement for Secretary of State Hillary Clinton, if she steps down as she has indicated.

But the committee's senior Republican, Saxby Chambliss of Georgia, said he doesn't think the issue is settled.

He said the concern is not whether the talking points were correct, but that Rice didn't go far enough.

"She knew at that point and time that al Qaeda was very likely responsible in part or in whole for the death of Ambassador Stevens," he said, intimating that Rice should have said that.

Another story that came out on the testimony of David Petraeus:

Gen. David Petraeus

The CIA knew terrorists attacked the U.S. embassy in Benghazi despite Obama administration claims it was not, former CIA Director David Petraeus said during closed-door testimony before a House investigating committee last week.

The testimony Petraeus gave directly contradicts the line given by the Obama administration – and one Petraeus himself repeated – that the attack was sparked by a spontaneous Muslim protest over a YouTube video mocking the Prophet Mohammed that spun out of control.

Behind closed doors on Capitol Hill, now-civilian Petraeus stressed to the House Foreign Affairs Committee that he always felt it was a terrorist attack, and that Al Queda related groups may have had a hand in it. But he also said that was unclear until key information, such as live security camera footage, came to the CIA over the days following the attack.

That information showed there was no demonstration and it was clearly a terrorist attack from the beginning to the end.

The initial story of a protest spun out of control unraveled shortly after the Obama administration launched a media offensive to establish that narrative. When it was revealed terrorist group Al Queada planned the assault to coincide with the anniversary of September 11, 2001, the CIA was blamed for refusing aid to the besieged embassy. The spy agency denied the charges, directly contradicting the White House. Two of the Americans killed during the attack were later revealed to be CIA agents, as were a large number of Americans on the ground at the site.

Susan Rice repeatedly said the attack was because Muslims were upset over an offensive YouTube video.

Congressional hearings in October revealed that not only was the State Department aware of several requests for increased security in Benghazi, the department rejected them.

The meeting did nothing to settle the argument on whether there was enough security at the consulate, or if the attack was actually preventable.

That debate divided along partisan lines during last week's hearing, with Republicans arguing there was not enough security, and Democrats insisting the situation was too unclear to determine proper levels of security.

Petraeus also told lawmakers that in his initial report, he declared there was "al Qaeda involvement." But that reference was stripped from his agency's original talking points.

White House national security council spokesman Ben Rhodes denied on Saturday the administration made any changes to the intelligence, reports *the Washington Times*, suggesting instead that the CIA itself altered the documents.

Other than changing change the word "consulate" to "diplomatic facility," the White House "worked off of the [talking] points that were provided by the intelligence community," Rhodes said. "So I can't speak to any other edits that may have been made within the intelligence community. I can't speak to what the process is within the CIA."

The issue of who changed the memo became a main issue following Petraeus' testimony, with top Republican lawmakers taking to the Sunday morning talk shows to make their case, reports *the Washington Times*.

Michigan Republican Congressman Mike Rogers blamed the White House's National Security Council Deputies Committee for altering an unclassified summary of what U.S intelligence knew of the attack.

Mike Rogers

Speaking on *Meet the Press*, Congressman Rogers said that the flow of information went from the CIA to the Committee, which is "populated by appointees from the [Obama] administration." It was there that the story changed from one of a terrorist attack to a protest that spun out of control, which U.S. Ambassador to the U.N. Susan E. Rice repeated over the following week.

"The narrative was wrong, and the intelligence was right," Congressman Rogers said.

Sen. Saxby Chambliss, vice chairman of the Senate Select Committee on Intelligence, blamed the changes on the National Security Council.

Ranking Democrats disputed Republican claims.

California Senator Diane Feinstein, chairwoman of the Senate Intelligence Committee, called Rep. Rogers' claim that the White House changed the narrative "false," adding it was still unclear who changed the "talking points."

Dianne Feinstein

She added that intelligence officials told her committee that the talking points were changed because it was not clear which groups had been involved in the consulate attack.

"The answer given to us is [U.S. intelligence agencies] didn't want to name a group until [they] had some certainty," the senator said.

According to intelligence officials, the talking-points changes removed the names of two extremist groups suspected in the attack — the Libyan Ansar al-Shariah militia and al Qaeda in the Islamic Maghreb, the terrorist network's affiliate in North Africa.

An intelligence official told *The Washington Times* that the changes also were intended to protect intelligence sources, because evidence of the groups' involvement came from highly classified electronic surveillance methods.

The September 11th assault on the U.S. consulate in Benghazi left U.S. Ambassador Chris Stevens and three other Americans dead. The government's precautions against such an attack, and its response when the American compound was overrun and burned, is now at the center of an increasingly bitter fight on Capitol Hill between President Barack Obama and his Democratic allies, on the one hand, and congressional Republicans.

Republican Congressman Peter King says the Obama administration's account of the terrorist attack in Benghazi was changed to delete any reference to al-Qaida involvement.

"As far as General Petraeus' testimony today was, that from the start, he had told us that this was a terrorist attack or that there were terrorists involved from the start. I told him in my questioning that I have a very different recollection of that. The clear impression that we were given was that the overwhelming evidence was that it arose out of spontaneous demonstrations," said King.

Yemeni protestors break a door of the U.S. Embassy during a protest about a film ridiculing Islam's Prophet Mohammed, Sana'a, Yemen, September 13, 2012.

2012

Petraeus returns to Fort Campbell to celebrate 70th anniversary

FORT CAMPBELL, Ky. (Aug. 17, 2012) -- Although rain clouds loomed over the Division Parade Field Friday morning, the 101st Airborne Division closed the "Week of the Eagles 2012: A History of Valor" with the traditional pass and review.

About 15,000 Soldiers and other tenant units gathered on the Division Parade Field for the pass and review by Division and Fort Campbell Commander, Maj. Gen. James C. McConville.

"This Division Review is a fitting end to a fabulous Week of the Eagles," McConville said. "It's important that we conduct this ceremony today. It's important because of our upcoming deployments. It will be a long time before we have this many Soldiers, colors and Guidons on the parade field before you."

Central Intelligence Agency Director David H. Petraeus returned to Fort Campbell to celebrate the Division's 70th anniversary.

"What a thrill it is to be back at this great post and among the magnificent troopers, past and present of the great 101st Airborne Division," said the retired four-star general who served as the 40th commander of the 101st and Fort Campbell.

In 2003, then-Maj. Gen. Petraeus led the 101st Airborne Division into Iraq during the first months of Operation Iraqi Freedom. He went on to lead Central Command and Multi-National Forces-Afghanistan before retiring from the U.S. Army in 2011. In September 2011, Petraeus became director of the CIA.

Petraeus lauded the 101st and its storied "Rendezvous with Destiny." He mentioned the 101st's storied history including Normandy on D-Day, Bastogne during World War II, the TET offensive in Vietnam, the invasions of Iraq and the ongoing pursuit of al-Qaida and the Taliban in Afghanistan.

"Indeed for 70 years, the Screaming Eagle patch has been a badge of honor worn by American Soldiers trained to respond quickly, skillfully and decisively in missions of the highest consequence," said Petraeus, who notably wore the patch on his uniform, even after leaving Fort Campbell.

"…the troopers of the great 101st have earned their place in the pantheon of those who have fought for America's freedoms, values and interests," he added.

This year's Week of the Eagles included several events, including the Toughest Air Assault Soldier Competition, 10k Fun Run Race, combatives and a memorial ceremony for the fallen.

The 2nd Brigade Combat Team brought home the Commander's Cup after winning most of the WoE competitions. Strike representatives received their trophy on the parade field.

"An amazing feat in its own right, but even more so considering much of the brigade's senior leadership is deployed to Afghanistan," McConville said, noting that 101st Sustainment Brigade's Lifeliners are also deployed to Afghanistan.

"Our 3rd Brigade 'Rakkasans' and our 101 CAB 'Destiny' begin their sixth deployment over the next couple of weeks," he added.

Both Petraeus and McConville noted the sacrifices made by Gold Star Families (those who have lost Soldiers in combat) and wounded warriors.

"The hard, but necessary consequence of this Division -- being among the first called into action when our nation must respond rapidly to challenges overseas," Petraeus said. "Your citizens owe each of you the utmost respect and deepest gratitude and we salute you -- all of you -- for your great service and sacrifice over the past decade."

Each speaker thanked the past veterans in the audience for paving the way for today's Army. "You have left us a history of valor, a proud legacy that we strive to live up to every day," McConville said. "You have made the 101st Airborne Division the most famous air assault division in the world. Thank you for what you have done."

Among the veterans in attendance was Leonard Kaminski, of Utah, who served with the 2nd Battalion, 501st Infantry Regiment, in Vietnam.

"It's like coming home again, almost," he said, about being at Fort Campbell.

Kaminski and a group of his former brothers in arms were among dozens of veterans who marched ahead of the active duty Soldiers during the review.

"It's an honor to lead the Division," he said. "I hope all these guys and girls out here will remember so they'll come back."

Ivan Worrell, a retired major from Sweetwater, Tenn., celebrated the Division's 70th anniversary with his fellow veterans who served in the 327th Infantry Regiment, 1st Brigade, in Vietnam.

A former 101st public information officer, Worrell said the 101st surpasses other Army divisions.

"Being a Screaming Eagle is something that a lot of people don't have the privilege of doing," he said. "It's the best unit in the Army. There's no better organization than the 101st."

Extramarital affair and resignation

David Petraeus and Paula Broadwell in July 2011

According to Petraeus associate Steven A. Boylan, Petraeus began an affair with Paula Broadwell, principal author of his biography, *All In: The Education of General David Petraeus*, in late 2011 when he was no longer an active duty military officer. Petraeus reportedly ended the affair in the summer of 2012, around the time that he learned that Broadwell had been sending harassing emails to a longstanding family friend of the Petraeus's, Jill Kelley.

Kelley, a Florida socialite who frequently entertained senior military personnel at her and her husband's Tampa mansion had approached an acquaintance who worked for the FBI Tampa Field Office in the late spring with regard to anonymous emails she considered threatening. The Bureau traced the emails to Broadwell, and noted that Broadwell appeared to be exchanging intimate messages with an email account belonging to Petraeus, which instigated an investigation into whether that account had been hacked into or was someone posing as Petraeus. According to an Associated Press report, rather than transmit emails to each other's inbox, which would have left a more obvious email trail, Petraeus and Broadwell left messages in a draft folder and the draft messages were then read by the other person when they logged into the same account.

Although US Attorney General Eric Holder was aware that the FBI had discovered the affair, it was not until November 6, 2012, that Petraeus' nominal superior, Director of National Intelligence James R. Clapper, was advised. That same evening Clapper called Petraeus and urged him to resign. Clapper notified the White House the next day, November 7. After being briefed on November 8, President Obama summoned Petraeus to the White House where Petraeus offered his resignation. Obama accepted his resignation on November 9, and Petraeus cited his affair when announcing that same day that he would resign as CIA Director.

Criticism after 2012 scandal

Petraeus had a strategy to influence military conditions by using the press relations effectively in the theater and in Washington, according to critics who assessed the general's military career after his fall from power. On November 13, 2012, Lawrence Korb, Ray McGovern, and Gareth Porter appearing on Al Jazeera English assessed the general's extensive military-media strategy linking his writings on counterguerrilla operations and subsequent military media efforts to his downfall with a female biographer. Critics observed that the Petraeus media strategy would prove damaging for American policy in the future because of the omissions and distorted interpretations that Washington policymakers, other experts, and the American public accepted from the highly effective Petraeus media contacts.

Military historians have noted the absence of field records for the Iraq and Afghanistan military campaigns, but have not personally been critical of the commanders in theater. One additional aspect of Petraeus' career that has come under increased scrutiny since his affair came to light has been his lack of a direct combat record in relation to the many awards he received. In particular, his Bronze Star Medal with Valor device has been mentioned in several media reports and questioned by several former Army officers.

David H. Petraeus Resignation Letter

Yesterday afternoon, I went to the White House and asked the President to be allowed, for personal reasons, to resign from my position as D/CIA. After being married for over 37 years, I showed extremely poor judgment by engaging in an extramarital affair. Such behavior is unacceptable, both as a husband and as the leader of an organization such as ours. This afternoon, the President graciously accepted my resignation.

As I depart Langley, I want you to know that it has been the greatest of privileges to have served with you, the officers of our Nation's Silent Service, a work force that is truly exceptional in every regard. Indeed, you did extraordinary work on a host of critical missions during my time as director, and I am deeply grateful to you for that.

Teddy Roosevelt once observed that life's greatest gift is the opportunity to work hard at work worth doing. I will always treasure my opportunity to have done that with you and I will always regret the circumstances that brought that work with you to an end.

Thank you for your extraordinary service to our country, and best wishes for continued success in the important endeavors that lie ahead for our country and our Agency.

With admiration and appreciation,

David H. Petraeus

Here are some newspaper reports from the resignation of David Petraeus

Petraeus Quits; Evidence of Affair Was Found by F.B.I.

Published: November 9, 2012

WASHINGTON — David H. Petraeus, the director of the Central Intelligence Agency and one of America's most decorated four-star generals, resigned on Friday after an F.B.I. investigation uncovered evidence that he had been involved in an extramarital affair.

David H. Petraeus is said to have had an affair with Paula Broadwell, right, who wrote a biography of him.

Mr. Petraeus issued a statement acknowledging the affair after President Obama accepted his resignation and it was announced by the C.I.A. The disclosure ended a triumphant re-election week for the president with an unfolding scandal.

Government officials said that the F.B.I. began an investigation into a "potential criminal matter" several months ago that was not focused on Mr. Petraeus. In the course of their inquiry into whether a computer used by Mr. Petraeus had been compromised, agents discovered evidence of the relationship as well as other security concerns. About two weeks ago, F.B.I. agents met with Mr. Petraeus to discuss the investigation.

Administration and Congressional officials identified the woman as Paula Broadwell, the co-author of a biography of Mr. Petraeus. Her book, "All In: The Education of General David Petraeus," was published this year. Ms. Broadwell could not be reached for comment.

Ms. Broadwell, a graduate of the United States Military Academy at West Point, spent 15 years in the military, according to a biography that had appeared on her Web site. She spent extended periods of time with Mr. Petraeus in Afghanistan, interviewing him for her book, which grew out of a two-year research project for her doctoral dissertation and which she promoted on a high-profile tour that included an appearance on "The Daily Show With Jon Stewart."

Married with two children, she has described Mr. Petraeus as her mentor.

Senior members of Congress were alerted to Mr. Petraeus's impending resignation by intelligence officials about six hours before the C.I.A. announced it. One Congressional official who was briefed on the matter said that Mr. Petraeus had been encouraged "to get out in front of the issue" and resign, and that he agreed.

As for how the affair came to light, the Congressional official said that "it was portrayed to us that the F.B.I. was investigating something else and came upon him. My impression is that the F.B.I. stumbled across this."

The Federal Bureau of Investigation did not inform the Senate and House Intelligence Committees about the inquiry until this week, according to Congressional officials, who noted that by law the panels — and especially their chairmen and ranking members — are supposed to be told about significant developments in the intelligence arena. The Senate committee plans to pursue the question of why it was not told, one official said.

The revelation of a secret inquiry into the head of the nation's premier spy agency raised urgent questions about Mr. Petraeus's 14-month tenure at the C.I.A. and the decision by Mr. Obama to elevate him to head the agency after leading the country's war effort in Afghanistan. White House officials said they did not know about the affair until this week, when Mr. Petraeus informed them.

"After being married for over 37 years, I showed extremely poor judgment by engaging in an extramarital affair," Mr. Petraeus said in his statement, expressing regret for his abrupt departure. "Such behavior is unacceptable, both as a husband and as the leader of an organization such as ours. This afternoon, the president graciously accepted my resignation."

Mr. Petraeus's admission and resignation represent a remarkable fall from grace for one of the most prominent figures in America's modern military and intelligence community, a commander who helped lead the nation's wartime activities in the decade after the Sept. 11 attacks and was credited with turning around the failing war effort in Iraq.

Mr. Petraeus almost single-handedly forced a profound evolution in the country's military thinking and doctrine with his philosophy of counterinsurgency, focused more on protecting the civilian population than on killing enemies. More than most of his flag officer peers, he understood how to navigate Washington politics and news media, helping him rise through the ranks and obtain resources he needed, although fellow Army leaders often resented what they saw as a grasping careerism.

"To an important degree, a generation of officers tried to pattern themselves after Petraeus," said Stephen Biddle, a military scholar at George Washington University who advised Mr. Petraeus at times. "He was controversial; a lot of people didn't like him. But everybody looked at him as the model of what a modern general was to be."

At the C.I.A., Mr. Petraeus maintained a low profile, in contrast to the celebrity that surrounded him as a general. But since the attack in Benghazi, Libya, that killed four Americans two months ago, critics had increasingly pressured him to give the agency's account of the chaotic night. Mr. Petraeus was scheduled to testify before a closed Congressional hearing next week.

White House officials say they were informed on Wednesday night that Mr. Petraeus was considering resigning because of an extramarital affair. Intelligence officials notified the president's national security staff. Mr. Obama at the time was on his way back to Washington from Chicago, where he had gone to receive election returns.

On Thursday morning, just before a staff meeting at the White House, Mr. Obama was told. "He was surprised, and he was disappointed," one senior administration official said. "You don't expect to hear that the Thursday after you were re-elected."

The president was in the White House all day on Thursday, getting back to his old routine after months on the campaign trail. That afternoon, Mr. Petraeus came in to see him, and informed him that he strongly believed he had to resign.

Mr. Obama did not accept his resignation right away. "He told him, 'I'll think about it overnight,' " the administration official said. After months on the road, the disclosure of a career-killing extramarital affair from his larger-than-life C.I.A. director was the last thing that Mr. Obama was expecting, the official said.

The president, officials said, did not want Mr. Petraeus to leave. But he ultimately decided that he would not lean heavily on him to stay. On Friday, he called Mr. Petraeus and accepted the resignation, "agreeing with Petraeus's judgment that he couldn't continue to lead the agency," a White House official said.

The White House had hoped to keep the news under wraps until after the daily briefing for the news media, but as it was reported on MSNBC, reporters checking their e-mail confronted Jay Carney, the press secretary, who tried to duck the questions.

"I think I'll let General Petraeus address this," Mr. Carney said. Shortly after the news broke, Mr. Obama released a statement praising Mr. Petraeus for his "extraordinary service" to the country and expressing support for him and his wife, Holly.

"By any measure, through his lifetime of service, David Petraeus has made our country safer and stronger," the president said. Without directly addressing the affair, Mr. Obama added, "Going forward, my thoughts and prayers are with Dave and Holly Petraeus, who has done so much to help military families through her own work."

A favorite of President George W. Bush and once the subject of intense speculation about his future as a possible presidential candidate, Mr. Petraeus managed the awkward move from a Republican administration to a Democratic one. He was one of the most telegenic faces of the military during his tenure, testifying frequently in Congress about the country's difficult battles overseas.

Mr. Petraeus clashed with Mr. Obama in 2008 during a campaign visit to Iraq, having what David Plouffe, his campaign manager, called in his book a "healthy debate" over troop levels in the country.

But the president's decision to tap Mr. Petraeus to command the war in Afghanistan, and later picking him to lead the C.I.A., effectively ended lingering concerns among Obama political advisers that the popular general might challenge his commander in chief during the election.

Mr. Petraeus and his wife met when he was a cadet at West Point; she was the daughter of the academy's superintendent and a student at Dickinson College in Pennsylvania.

Holly Petraeus works for the Consumer Financial Protection Bureau, running a branch dedicated to educating military families about financial matters and monitoring their consumer complaints.

Mr. Petraeus's resignation and the circumstances surrounding it stunned military officers who have served alongside him in war zones over the past two decades and the national security establishment he later served.

"It was a punch in the gut for those of us who know him," said Col. Michael J. Meese, a professor at West Point who has known Mr. Petraeus for a decade and served as one of his top aides in Bosnia, Iraq and Afghanistan.

"Dave's decision to step down represents the loss of one of our nation's most respected public servants." James R. Clapper, the director of national intelligence, said in a statement.

By acknowledging an extramarital affair, Mr. Petraeus, 60, was confronting a sensitive issue for a spy chief. Intelligence agencies are often concerned about the possibility that agents who engage in such behavior could be blackmailed for information.

Mr. Petraeus praised his colleagues at the C.I.A.'s headquarters in Langley, Va., calling them "truly exceptional in every regard" and thanking them for their service to the country. He made it clear that his departure was not how he had envisioned ending a storied career in the military and in intelligence.

"Teddy Roosevelt once observed that life's greatest gift is the opportunity to work hard at work worth doing," he said. "I will always treasure my opportunity to have done that with you, and I will always regret the circumstances that brought that work with you to an end."

Under Mr. Bush, Mr. Petraeus was credited for helping to develop and put in place the "surge" in troops in Iraq that helped wind down the war there. Mr. Petraeus was moved to Afghanistan in 2010 after Mr. Obama fired Gen. Stanley A. McChrystal over comments he made to a reporter.

In his statement on Friday, Mr. Obama said that Michael J. Morell, the deputy director of the C.I.A., would take over once again as acting director, as he did briefly after Leon E. Panetta left the agency last year.

Among those who might succeed Mr. Petraeus permanently is John O. Brennan, the president's adviser for domestic security and counterterrorism. Mr. Brennan was considered for C.I.A. director before Mr. Obama's term began but withdrew amid criticism from some of the president's liberal supporters. Another possibility is Michael G. Vickers, the top Pentagon intelligence policy official and a former C.I.A. paramilitary officer.

Reporting was contributed by Peter Baker, Helene Cooper, Michael S. Schmidt, Eric Schmitt and Scott Shane.

This article has been revised to reflect the following correction:

Correction: November 9, 2012

An earlier version of this article incorrectly stated that David H. Petraeus was expected to remain in President Obama's cabinet. The C.I.A. director is not a cabinet member in the Obama administration.

A version of this article appeared in print on November 10, 2012, on page A1 of the New York edition with the headline: Petraeus Resigns at C.I.A.; F.B.I. Discovered an Affair.

The Rise and Fall of `General Peaches'

Nov. 14, 2012

The call, from one retired four-star general to another, was somber. Just-departed CIA chief Dave Petraeus' voice – usually assertive, buffed by optimism — was lower, slower and more subdued than his former comrade had ever heard.

"I really screwed up," he told Jack Keane, a retired four-star general — like Petraeus — who stepped down as the Army's No. 2 officer in 2003. "This is my fault, and I'm devastated by the pain and suffering that I've caused."

No kidding. But this is the rest of the story of "General Peaches," whose career reached its apogee turning the Iraq war around in 2007, and whose professional and personal lives crashed and burned last Friday when he acknowledged an extra-marital affair, resigning from government service for the first time since he arrived at West Point as a cadet in 1970.

"Peaches" was the nickname Petraeus picked up as a kid when pals found "Petraeus" too tough to say. Over the past decade, many Americans, in and out of uniform, learned how to say "Petraeus." Most journalists even learned how to spell it.

Fellow four-stars felt Petraeus' pain after he acknowledged his affair Friday with a woman identified as Paula Broadwell, a fellow West Pointer (*he, Class of '74; she, Class of '95*) and author of *All In: The Education of General David Petraeus*. Some of those who retired at lower ranks, not so much.

"I don't think this personal indiscretion, in and of itself, could possibly trump his achievements and accomplishments," says Keane, one-time Army vice chief of staff and a key architect, as a retired four-star general, of the Iraq surge led by Petraeus. "It's comparable to what World War II generals achieved."

"Great soldier, statesman and patriot," Peter Chiarelli, the Army's No. 2 officer until earlier this year, says. "He and his wonderful family are in our thoughts and prayers."

"He is one of the most talented and dedicated officers we have produced since World War II," says Barry McCaffrey, who ran U.S. Southern Command before retiring with four stars in 2001. "I have known him since he was a captain. From the start Dave saw the whole picture and had the moral courage and leadership to finally get the armed forces on the right strategy in Iraq. His tactical and political cleverness pulled us back from a disaster."

But not everyone sang Petraeus' praises. "Petraeus is a remarkable piece of fiction created and promoted by neocons in government, the media and academia," argues Douglas Macgregor, a retired and outspoken Army colonel and innovator, known for *Breaking the Phalanx*, his book taking the Army to task for the way it organizes and uses its ground forces.

Macgregor elaborates:

"How does an officer with no personal experience of direct fire combat in Panama or Desert Storm become a division CDR in 2003, man who for 35 years shamelessly reinforced whatever dumb idea his superior advanced regardless of its impact on soldiers, let alone the nation, a man who served repeatedly as a sycophantic aide-de-camp, military assistant and executive officer to four stars get so far? How does the same man who balked at closing with and destroying the enemy in 2003 in front of Baghdad agree to sacrifice more than a thousand American lives and destroy thousands of others installing Iranian national power in Baghdad with a surge that many in and out of uniform warned against? Then, how does this same man repeat the self-defeating tactics one more time in Afghanistan? The answer is simple: Petraeus was always a useful fool in the Leninist sense for his political superiors — Wolfowitz, Rumsfeld, and Gates. And that is precisely how history will judge him."

As noted, Macgregor can be outspoken.

Ralph Peters is another blunt-speaking retired Army officer and author. "When a man becomes more reputation than substance, his reputation had better be invulnerable," he said of Petraeus' plight. "Every successful man has encountered at least one Paula Broadwell. The smart ones don't take her calls."

THE RISE OF GENERAL PETRAEUS

Petraeus grew up just up the Hudson River from the U.S. Military Academy at West Point, the son of a Dutch sea captain and his librarian wife. As one of the nation's leading Army officers, he combined his father's globe-girdling sense of adventure with his mother's bookish brains.

He knew how to cozy up to powerful military mentors even as a young cadet at the U.S. Military Academy at West Point: he began dating Hollister Knowlton, the daughter of the academy's superintendent, before his 1974 graduation and commissioning as a 2nd lieutenant in the U.S. Army.

Lieut. General William Knowlton served as superintendent at West Point from 1970 1974, matching Petraeus' time there as a student. Petraeus' father-in-law became perhaps his first important Army mentor: a veteran of four World War II military campaigns, he would go on to serve on the staffs of Army generals – and legends — Omar Bradley and Dwight D. Eisenhower (he died in 2008, 28 years after retiring from the Army).

"A striver to the max," Petraeus' yearbook said, "Dave was always 'going for it' in sports, academics, leadership, and even his social life." He and Holly married two months after his graduation. They have two children; a son — now serving his second Army tour in Afghanistan — and a daughter, married last month.

Petraeus' self-discipline was legendary, even in the military where discipline is an everyday trait. That makes his fall from grace all the more startling to former comrades. After a decade of admirably commanding U.S. troops in the nation's two post-9/11 wars, the revelation of his acknowledged affair with Broadwell was like a Wallenda suddenly and surprisingly slipping without benefit of a net.

Petraeus was a buzz saw through the Army's ranks during the first decade of the 21st Century. As a major general, he led the 101st Airborne to Mosul in firefights along the Euphrates River to great acclaim in 2003. He spoke up when he felt he needed to. "He was pretty good at being a constructive critic within the system," says Michael O'Hanlon, a long-time friend and military scholar at the Brookings Institution. "When [Coalition Provisional Authority chief] Paul Bremer disbanded the Iraqi army with the support of [senior Pentagon civilian in Iraq] Walt Slocombe, Petraeus challenged them. He said, 'You guys are creating enemies for me.'

Maj. Gen. David H. Petraeus, commander of the 101st Airborne Division, and Ghamin Al Basso, governor of Ninevah Province, cut a cake to celebrate the activation of Iraqi security units in Mosul in January 2004.

"This was a potentially fatal mistake and it needed to be addressed and confronted directly. Petraeus proved his willingness to take some personal risk for the good of the mission," O'Hanlon adds. "He was saying things these people did not want to hear and they did not know he was about to become the most famous four-star general of the modern era. At the time, he was just one of their two-stars who had a reputation for speaking his mind, perhaps more than some people preferred."

Petraeus' appeal was international. "Very shortly after he arrived, we're looking out the window of the Saddam's Republican Palace and out the back there was this growing trailer park," recalls British Brigadier General Nigel Aylwin-Foster, who was Petraeus' deputy in training the Iraq military in 2004 in Baghdad. "He pointed to the trailer nearest our window and the entrance we used to get into the building. He told me that he was going to get his aide to arrange for him to have that trailer because it meant that he wouldn't have to waste so much time getting from the trailer to work. That's only a small little detail, but it exemplifies to me just how he would do everything he could to just get on with work."

Another recollection: "He never came to breakfast – he had it brought to his desk – he didn't want to waste any time."

Petraeus raised eyebrows — in the Pentagon and elsewhere — when he penned an op-ed column for the *Washington Post* in September 2004 advocating his train-and-equip mission for the Iraqi military. It was basically pablum, but it was *political* pablum. It showed his willingness to color outside the lines.

When he didn't slam-dunk the training assignment, he jumped at the chance in his follow-on three-star billet: to rewrite the Army's counter-insurgency manual. He quickly moved on to the Army's Command and General Staff College at Fort Leavenworth, Kan. – long viewed as a backwater – to do just that.

"He learned from failure," O'Hanlon says. "Because when he was lieutenant general there in Iraq, as head of the training command, it didn't go so well. It taught him that giving the Iraqis technical skills and equipment wasn't going to trump their political divisions if you could deal with those."

PETRAEUS' PEAK

From CGSC at Fort Leavenworth, he got to apply the retooled manual's people-centric precepts as a full four-star general back in Iraq, where it succeeded as a part of the 2007 "surge" of 30,000 additional U.S. troops into the country over the objections of more traditional officers. Petraeus' career crested when he led the surge and helped turn what had been a civil war between Sunnis and Shiites into episodic bombings and assassinations that continue to this day.

Keane cites Petraeus's 2007 arrival in Iraq – for a third tour there – as the peak a military career studded with successes. "A lot of people truly did not understand how far the war in Iraq had gone in terms of our failure," Keane says. "Iraq was clearly a fractured state and about to go off the cliff, we were in the throes of suffering a humiliating defeat." (Ironically – and perhaps in an indictment of the way the country selects its leaders — Petraeus' predecessor in Iraq, General George Casey, was awarded with the plum assignment as Army chief of staff after leaving Baghdad).

"While many people wanted more troops in Iraq, he knew we needed a new strategy; more troops using the old strategy, you still fail," Keane says. "Just saying it's a new strategy is one thing, but actually changing what all the troops were doing is quite significant. The strategy he put in place was to protect the population by bringing the troops out from the big bases and employing them at the platoon level in Iraqi neighborhoods, where they would eat, sleep and patrol day and night."

Gen. David Petraeus heads to a UH-60 Blackhawk helicopter with then-Sen. Barack Obama after the senator's July 2008 arrival at Baghdad International Airport.

Of course, rejiggering a strategy is only half the fight. "To get an Army that's already fighting a war to change in stride to a total different military strategy on the ground, and to get everybody on the same page – was accomplished by the sheer force of Dave Petraeus' will," Keane says. "He changed the attitude in the multi-national headquarters he was now commanding, almost overnight, by convincing them, that despite the fact we were indeed losing this war, it was not hopeless and that we can win, and we would win. He believed it himself, and he communicated that confidence to them."

President Bush tapped him to head U.S. Central Command in 2008 – one of the military's top assignments. (He also drove the Pentagon crazy by repeatedly dealing directly with Petraeus and calling him "Dave".) His selection represented a kick in the teeth to old-school Army officers and their vanishing dreams of massive tank battles and artillery skirmishes (some of whom privately called Petraeus "King David" for his high self-regard and chumminess with reporters and other alien life forms).

The choice made clear that then-defense secretary Robert Gates wanted commanders able to carry out the messy, irregular kind of combat championed by Petraeus that Gates saw the U.S. fighting for years to come. It reinforced the message the defense chief had just delivered to young Air Force and Army officers, where he criticized their leaders for devoting too much time and effort to future potential wars, and not enough to the real wars now underway.

"The kinds of conflicts that we're doing, not just in Iraq but in Afghanistan, and some of the challenges that we face elsewhere in the region and in the Central Command area, are very much characterized by asymmetric warfare," Gates said shortly after the White House announced Petraeus' nomination. "And I don't know anybody in the United States military better qualified to lead that effort."

But Petraeus' sure-footedness escaped him in July 2009 when he made the Air Force the butt of one of his jokes. Speaking to an annual Marine Corps Association Foundation dinner, Petraeus praised the leathernecks while taking tongue-in-cheek shots at both his own service and the Air Force. "A soldier is trudging through the muck in the midst of a downpour with a 60-pound rucksack on his back. `This is tough, he thinks to himself,'" Petraeus began. "Just ahead of him trudges an Army Ranger with an 80-pound pack on his back. `This is really tough,' he thinks. And ahead of him is a Marine with a 90-pound pack on, and he thinks to himself, `I love how tough this is,'" Petraeus said to appreciative cheers from his audience.

U.S. Central Command chief Army General David Petraeus testifies on Capitol Hill in March 2010

"Then, of course, 30,000 feet above them, an Air Force pilot flips aside his ponytail," he added to howls of laughter and applause from the Marines. "I'm sorry — I don't know how that got in there — I know they haven't had ponytails in a year or two — and looks down at them through his cockpit as he flies over. `Boy,' he radios his wingman, `it must be tough down there.'"

Although Petraeus quickly added "all joking aside," the collateral damage was already done. Air Force partisans got wind of the comments made by the chief of the U.S. Central Command and tracked them down to the Marine Corps Association website. It contained a copy of Petraeus' prepared remarks — including the ponytail crack — and a video of his talk. The Air Force Association daily newsletter called Petraeus' remarks "beyond outrageous" and said they "belittled the contributions of the Air Force to the joint force." The association, a non-profit educational group that supports the service, said the comment is "symptomatic of the long-held belief of many ground commanders that airpower is no longer, if it ever was, relevant." The episode showed that, despite his skills and education, sometimes Petraeus was tone-deaf.

He remained at Central Command until Army General Stan McChrystal's staff forced their boss out of a job by speaking ill of their civilian masters in June 2010. President Obama fired McChrystal and Petraeus effectively took a demotion to replace him as commander of the Afghan campaign.

MISSING THE BRASS RING

Petraeus had always wanted to come back before the Senate Armed Services Committee for a third confirmation hearing. But he was hoping it would be for promotion to serve as chairman of the Joint Chiefs of Staff — not a demotion to run one of two wars he had been overseeing as chief of U.S. Central Command.

Obama and his camp had been somewhat leery of Petraeus — there was just a whiff of desperation in the air when they tapped him to succeed McChrystal – and the stakes couldn't have been higher. When Bush signed off on Petraeus' plan for the Iraq surge, the President was near the end of his second term. This time around, Obama was left to wonder if he could win a second term, and Petraeus suddenly loomed large in his re-election hopes.

Obama was determined to keep Petraeus at arms-length, several links away in the chain of command. Pentagon officials exulted at the change; there would be far less direct communication between the commander-in-chief and his most famous commander.

When he assumed command in Afghanistan, Petraeus' pragmatic side came into view: he stepped up attacks on the Taliban and worried less about protecting civilians, the key tenet of the counter-insurgency manual he helped revise.

On April 28, 2011, President Obama announced that General David Petraeus would hang up his uniform and take the reins at the CIA.

But such practicality only took him so far. Pentagon official say the Obama White House dashed Petraeus' goal of serving as chairman of the Joint Chiefs of Staff – the nation's top military officer – out of fear he would seek to slow down the U.S. troop pullout from Afghanistan. Instead, he ended up — out of uniform — running the CIA.

PETRAEUS' PERSONALITY

Petraeus seemed different from most Army generals, and he was. In addition to his West Point education, he attended the Army's Command and General Staff College, taught at West Point, and earned a Princeton Ph.D. in international relations in 1987. While he never brandished his education as a weapon, he wielded it as a tool to burnish his evolving reputation as the nation's pre-eminent post-9/11 military commander.

He was like the kid saving for a new and costly bike: he bided his time, toiling in anonymity – but close to power — carrying bags for Army generals like NATO commander John Galvin, Army chief of staff Carl Vuono, and Henry Shelton, chairman of the Joint Chiefs. Some colleagues criticized him for spending too much time with the brass, and not enough with the troops.

Petraeus, who in person seemed to be a coiled spring perpetually under tension, didn't hide his ambition. It burned brightly, and kept him from becoming close friends with many comrades. Instead, he relied on a coterie of junior officers, many of whom had served multiple tours with him in Iraq and Afghanistan over the past decade.

Nor did he fit the mold of a traditional back-slapping, *hale-fellow-well-met* Army officer. Instead, he had the aura of a cerebral general, a whip-smart but somewhat aloof commander who knew – or at least you suspected he believed – that he was the smartest guy in the war room.

PETRAEUS' LEGACY

He raised eyebrows when he invited outsiders into his war rooms to question strategy and sent them out in military aircraft as professional second-guessers.

"The man has always been controversial, and therefore his legacy was going to be controversial," says Stephen Biddle, a military expert at George Washington University and the Council on Foreign Relations who served on three Petraeus advisory teams – one for Afghanistan, one for Iraq, and one when the general took over Central Command.

Biddle fears the lack of any formal review of the U.S. military's successes and failures in the post-9/11 wars will make Petraeus' fall from grace cast a long shadow over the conflicts.

"It's interesting that the Army, and the military in general, is not doing a big formal review of what went well and what went badly since 2001 — not in the sense of what we did after World War II and the Strategic Bombing Survey, or that the Air Force did after 1991," says Biddle. "If you're not going to do this formally, it's going to happen in hallway conversations – informally.

And this kind of thing could have a bigger impact on hallway-conversation corporate memory than it would on a formal study.

"You can't make a rigorous argument that whether Dave Petraeus had an affair leaving the military should affect the way we think about counter-insurgency – there's no logical connection there at all," Biddle says. "And yet, it's probably going to affect people's perception of the man, and you can imagine if the primary way the military comes to grips with its experience is in informal, person-to-person conversation, that this could have the effect of weakening his advocacy and strengthening his detractors."

Biddle is stunned by what happened. "Petraeus is one of the most disciplined humans who ever walked the face of the Earth, and it's certainly very surprising that this happened to him," he says. "I find the analogy to John Edwards kind of interesting, personally," he adds, referring to the North Carolina senator and 2008 Democratic presidential candidate and his videographer, Rielle Hunter. "Here are two very accomplished, very ambitious, very self-aware people, who both fell for their biographer. A certain degree of narcissism looked like it had something to do with both men's falls."

O'Hanlon of Brookings also advised Petraeus while he was still in uniform, and attended graduate school with him at Princeton. He says Petraeus represented that minority of military officers willing to challenge the system, instead of merely muddling along.

"The respect for tradition – the old general with the drawl and the tough guy and not necessarily the biggest intellect – that has probably been, more often than not, the stereotypical Army leader," O'Hanlon says. "Petraeus was the opposite – he was brilliant, he was slightly iconoclastic – not to the point of being suicidal, but to the point of being willing to challenge prevailing ideas once he felt there was a strong case to do so – and he did it politely, professionally and in a politically savvy way."

Two accidents nearly killed Petraeus: in 1991, a soldier tripped, discharging his M-16 that fired a slug into Petraeus' chest, and nine years later his parachute collapsed when he was 60 feet off the ground, smashing his pelvis. But he remained – and remains – in excellent shape, out-running younger officers in his final Army tours with 6-minute miles.

"I learned very early on you don't go running with General Petraeus," recalls Aylwin-Foster, his 2004 deputy in Baghdad. "'He kept on saying to me, `Nigel we've got to get you out for a run.' We're all fit in the army, but people had warned me: if he invites you out for a run, just find a reason not to do it because you'll start off at a little jog, chatting away about whatever, and then a few miles later he's just getting faster and faster and faster." So Aylwin-Foster never ran with Petraeus.

Some former senior officers fret over the gap Petraeus' sudden departure signals. "It breaks my heart," says retired Army major general Robert Scales, a military historian, Petraeus friend and former head of the Army War College. "Over the last 10 years, whenever Dave showed up, the right grand operational solution seems to have taken hold," Scales says. "I believed that happened in 2003 in Iraq, in 2006-07, again in Iraq, and I believe it began to happen again in Afghanistan.

General David Petraeus arrives at his Senate CIA confirmation hearing in June 2011 behind his wife, Holly, as his biographer, Paula Broadwell, second from the left, looks on.

"It couldn't happen at a worse time," Scales says. "Here we are, intentionally creating a military vacuum. I don't think anybody's given a lot of thought to what the impact of this is – to have Petraeus walk away from the CIA at this time. Dave walks away with a unique set of skills and knowledge and associations and wisdom and historical depth and understanding of the region and the people that I don't think any civilian can replicate, at least not any time soon."

Speaking of history, Jack Keane pauses after comparing Petraeus to the nation's World War II generals. "He didn't fight a big war like they did," he acknowledges. "But he took a war in Iraq where we were about to lose and turned it around. And he began to do the same in Afghanistan. Very few generals have achieved that distinction."

The White House

Office of the Press Secretary

For Immediate Release
November 09, 2012

Statement by President Obama on the Resignation of CIA Director David Petraeus

David Petraeus has provided extraordinary service to the United States for decades. By any measure, he was one of the outstanding General officers of his generation, helping our military adapt to new challenges, and leading our men and women in uniform through a remarkable period of service in Iraq and Afghanistan, where he helped our nation put those wars on a path to a responsible end. As Director of the Central Intelligence Agency, he has continued to serve with characteristic intellectual rigor, dedication, and patriotism. By any measure, through his lifetime of service David Petraeus has made our country safer and stronger.

Today, I accepted his resignation as Director of the Central Intelligence Agency. I am completely confident that the CIA will continue to thrive and carry out its essential mission, and I have the utmost confidence in Acting Director Michael Morell and the men and women of the CIA who work every day to keep our nation safe. Going forward, my thoughts and prayers are with Dave and Holly Petraeus, who has done so much to help military families through her own work. I wish them the very best at this difficult time.

2013 and later

On March 28, 2013, Petraeus joined the American Corporate Partners (ACP), a national nonprofit organization that connects post-9/11 veterans to business professionals for career guidance. American Corporate Partners (ACP; www.acp-usa.org) is a New York-based national nonprofit organization founded in 2008 to address veterans' career transition needs through two free programs: a nationwide veteran mentoring program, and an online network, ACP AdvisorNet (www.acp-advisornet.org), offering career, employment and small business advice through a Q&A platform. In March 2013, Petraeus has accepted the role of Honorary Chairmen of the OSS Society.

Petraeus was named a visiting professor at Macaulay Honors College at the City University of New York in July 2013. According to a statement from Petraeus, "I look forward to leading a seminar at Macaulay that examines the developments that could position the United States - and our North American partners - to lead the world out of the current global economic slowdown." After his anticipated $200,000 salary for the academic year drew fire from critics, Petraeus agreed to take on the teaching position for just $1 in order to keep the focus on the students and away from any monetary controversy. In September 2013 Petraeus was harassed by students at CUNY while walking on campus.

Macaulay Honors College at the City University of New York

In September 2013 Petraeus was harassed by students at CUNY while walking on campus.

UPDATE: College students harass retired Gen. David Petraeus

In one of the most sickening displays of disrespect toward a veteran since the Vietnam War, students swore at and harassed retired Army Gen. David Petraeus, who recently began teaching a class at the City University of New York.

A video posted on YouTube titled "CUNY Students Confront War Criminal David Petraeus" shows Petraeus walking through a gauntlet of students who aggressively taunt him for close to 90 seconds.

"There's blood all over you, I can smell it," one student yells.

Petraeus, who served as the top U.S. commander in both Iraq and Afghanistan, takes the abuse stoically despite attempts by the students to provoke him.

It is not clear if the taunting continued after the end of the video.

UPDATED: Ann Kirschner, dean of the Macaulay Honors College at CUNY, has issued a statement about the protests:

"Our university is a place where complex issues and points of view across the political and cultural spectrum are considered and debated in the hopes that we might offer solutions to the problems in our world. In order to advance reasoned debate on such issues, it is important that multiple points of view be heard.

"Great universities strive to connect their students with remarkable leaders and thinkers so students can examine a variety of ideas, debate them, and form their own opinions. Those perspectives find expression through discussion in and out of the classroom.

"We may disagree, but we must always do so in a spirit of mutual respect and understanding. While the college supports the articulation of all points of view on critical issues, it is essential that dialogue within the academic setting always be conducted civilly."

CUNY students being arrested by police during the Petraeus protest

CUNY students being arrested by police during the Petraeus protest

Arrested CUNY 6 spark debate and continued protest against Gen. Petraeus

The University Faculty Senate (UFS), the faculty governance body for university-wide academic matters, put out a similar statement defending Petraeus' right to teach, saying, "Because they disagree with Professor Petraeus' views, these demonstrators intend to deprive him of his ability to teach and the ability of his students to learn from him. CUNY has long-established policies to protect the academic freedom of faculty, which are essential for the university's operation as a center of learning."

But not all of the university's recognition of the protests have been so supportive of Petraeus.

Many professors, who are represented by the UFS, responded to their statement with shock.

"I am shocked and disappointed at the UFS statement, which effectively questions the right of CUNY students and faculty to express their views about a highly controversial public figure who was given a privileged platform to express his views in the CUNY community," wrote Tom Angotti, professor of urban affairs and planning at Hunter College and the Graduate Center in a comment. "As someone who has taught in the Macaulay Honors program, I am ashamed to see Petraeus there, and as long as he is there, I will be absent."

CUNY's Professional Staff Congress, the union representing faculty and professional staff at CUNY, came out in support of its students. It unanimously passed a statement calling for a formal investigation of the NYPD's use of force and is calling for the city to drop all charges against the protestors.

City College Students for Educational Rights has a Mr.Zine petition that has been signed by over 500 people, including CUNY alums, students, professors and the like from colleges and universities around the world. It reads, "We emphatically support the efforts of these CUNY students to resist the attempts by the U.S. government and the CUNY administration to turn the university into an infamous war college with the appointment of Petraeus."

Here is the Mr. Zine petition

Note: I excluded the signatures

Statement of Support to CUNY Students Attacked and Arrested in Peaceful Protests Against Ex-Gen. David Petraeus

On September 18, 2013, a press release issued by the Ad Hoc Committee Against the Militarization of CUNY stated: "Six students were arrested in a brutal, unprovoked police attack during a peaceful protest by the City University of New York's students and faculty against CUNY's appointment of former CIA chief ex-General David Petraeus. Students were punched, slammed against vehicles and against the pavement by police captains and officers, after the NYPD forced them off the pavement and onto the street."

As graduate students and educators of CUNY, we express our outrage at the violent and unprovoked actions by the NYPD against CUNY students peacefully protesting the appointment of war criminal David Petraeus as a lecturer at the Macaulay Honors College. We deplore the use of violence and brutal tactics against CUNY students and faculty who were protesting outside the college. It is unacceptable for the university to allow the police to violently arrest students.

We emphatically support the efforts of these CUNY students to resist the attempts by the U.S. government and the CUNY administration to turn the university into an infamous "war college" with the appointment of Petraeus. Petraeus is responsible for countless deaths and innumerable destruction in Iraq and Afghanistan as a war commander and chief of the CIA. Although resigning from his position as CIA director in November, Petraeus has continued his involvement in U.S. foreign policy. Most recently Petraeus has called on Congress to back a military strike on Syria, stating "failure of Congress to approve the president's request would have serious ramifications not just in the Mideast but around the world." His current roles as "adjunct" lecturer at CUNY and professor at USC speak to the increasing U.S. military and state security involvement within higher education.

We call on CUNY to terminate Petraeus' appointment and to ask for the charges against these students to be dropped immediately.

Signed,

Members of the Ad Hoc Committee, including those who were arrested, have said the group will continue to protest at every one of Petraeus' classes until both ROTC and Petraeus are out of the entire system. Other groups have also picked up the call to end the militarization of CUNY, with the Free University, a group of students and professors conducting free courses in New York. They have been holding bi-weekly "counter classes" directly after Petraeus' Monday courses to "counter his course with critical education of our own."

Petraeus drops all the charges of the CUNY 6

A comment from the Author:

As a military Veteran I would just like to add my personal opinion here.

I believe all American citizens have the right to protest against something that they do not agree with. I just hope that one day, these six students will come to realize that the man that they were protesting against…

"Is one of the soldiers who fought to protect that right to protest."

General Petraeus named Judge Widney Professor at USC

On May 1, 2013, the University of Southern California named Petraeus as a Judge Widney Professor, "a title reserved for eminent individuals from the arts, sciences, professions, business and community and national leadership."

Retired Gen. David Petraeus addresses ROTC students during his recent tour of USC.

May 2, 2013

Retired Gen. David Petraeus, architect and namesake of the counterinsurgency doctrine that stabilized Iraq under U.S. and allied forces and former director of the CIA, will join the USC faculty this fall.

Petraeus, whose appointment becomes effective on July 1, will be a Judge Widney Professor, a title reserved for eminent individuals from the arts, sciences, professions, business, and community and national leadership. Judge Robert Maclay Widney was USC's founder.

"USC is thrilled to have General Petraeus join our faculty as a Judge Widney Professor," said President C. L. Max Nikias. "He embodies all the noble qualities of our founder along with a fearless commitment to excellence. His presence will have a profound impact on our students across many disciplines."

Petraeus will spend time at USC each academic semester teaching classes, participating in seminars and panels, engaging in working sessions with students and faculty, and mentoring student veterans and ROTC members.

His varied research interests include the leadership of the United States in revolutionizing energy, information technology, life sciences and manufacturing. He is also interested in exploring whether such leadership heralds the start of what he calls the "North American Decades."

"I am very grateful to have an opportunity to be part of a great university that prizes academic excellence, that is doing cutting-edge research in areas of enormous importance to our country, and that is known for steadfast support of its veterans and ROTC programs," Petraeus said.

Petraeus' appointment includes affiliations with the USC School of Social Work, including the program in military social work; the USC Price School of Public Policy; the USC Annenberg School for Communication and Journalism, including the program in public diplomacy; the USC Dornsife College of Letters, Arts and Sciences, including the Department of International Relations; the USC Viterbi School of Engineering, including the Information Sciences Institute; the USC Institute for Creative Technologies; and the USC Libraries, including the USC Sidney Harman Academy for Polymathic Study.

"The appointment of General Petraeus as a Judge Widney Professor at USC will add transformative energy to our teaching and research in international relations, government, economics, management, defense studies and military science — fields mastered by this clear-thinking jargon-free polymath," said University Professor and noted California historian Kevin Starr.

Petraeus served as director of the CIA from September 2011 until November 2012. Prior to assuming the directorship, he was a highly decorated four-star general, serving more than 37 years in the U.S. Army before retiring in August 2011.

A lauded combat leader and strategist, Petraeus was instrumental in reshaping American military tactics through his focus on the concepts of a comprehensive civil-military counterinsurgency campaign. At Petraeus' retirement ceremony from the Army, Adm. Michael Mullen, former chairman of the Joint Chiefs of Staff, compared Petraeus to Ulysses S. Grant, John J. Pershing, George Marshall and Dwight D. Eisenhower as one of the great battle captains of American history.

Petraeus' final assignment in the military was as commander of the NATO International Security Assistance Force and U.S. forces in Afghanistan. Other assignments included his service as the 10th commander of the U.S. Central Command, where he was responsible for military operations in Afghanistan, Pakistan, Central Asia, the Arabian Peninsula, Iraq, the Levant and Egypt — and his service as commanding general of the Multi-National Force-Iraq for more than 19 months.

"For the past 37 years, General Petraeus has served our country as a dedicated public servant and remarkable leader," said Jack H. Knott, dean of USC Price. "Given our school's focus on government and public policy, as well as the academic administrative home for the ROTC program at USC, it is a particular honor for us to have General Petraeus join the USC faculty."

Petraeus earned a bachelor's degree from the U.S. Military Academy, from which he graduated in 1974 as a distinguished cadet, finishing in the top 5 percent of his class. He later received the General George C. Marshall Award as the top graduate of the U.S. Army Command and General Staff College class of 1983. He subsequently earned an MPA and a PhD in international relations from the Woodrow Wilson School of Public and International Affairs at Princeton University. He served as assistant professor of international relations at West Point and also completed a fellowship at Georgetown University.

The president of the Currahee Board of Trustees announced May 6, 2013, that Petraeus agreed to serve on the board of trustees that perserves Camp Toccoa. During WWII, four of the main parachute infantry regiments of the Army trained at Camp Toccoa prior to their deployment.

Kohlberg Kravis Roberts & Co. L.P., a New York investment firm, hired Petraeus as chairman of the firm's newly created KKR Global Institute in May 2013. Petraeus will support its investment teams and portfolio companies when studying new investments, especially in new locations.

Team Rubicon, an organization that focuses individuals with military experience and first responders to deploy emergency response teams announced on June 18, 2013, that Petraeus has joined its board of advisors.

Royal United Services Institute (RUSI) named Petraeus as a Senior Vice President of the organization in August 2013. According to RUSI, "The honorary role was created by RUSI's trustees and advisory council in recognition of General Petraeus' long association with the Institute and his distinguished contribution to the study and development of defence and international security concepts, as well as his implementation of those concepts in operations in the Balkans, Iraq, and Afghanistan".

Petraeus will take a new job with investment firm Kohlberg Kravis Roberts & Co. L.P. He will serve as chairman of the New York firm's newly created KKR Global Institute. Victor Davis Hanson has authored *The Savior Generals* focusing on five generals from the past. According to Ed Driscoll, "these men range from Themistocles and Belisarius to the Civil War's General Sherman, Matthew Ridgway, in Korea and David Petraeus in Iraq. They became "savior generals" in VDH's estimation, because each salvaged a war that appeared to have been hopelessly lost by a previous general whose name and ego caused him to make a hash of the fight."

In October, Petraeus joins the Harvard's John F. Kennedy School of Government as a non-resident senior fellow at the Belfer Center for Science and International Affairs. According to the school, Petraeus will jointly lead a new project focusing on the technological, scientific and economic dynamics that are spurring renewed North American competitiveness. "The Coming

North America Decades" project will analyze how potential policy choices could effect this ongoing transformation.

Recognitions and honors

Decorations and badges

Petraeus' decorations and badges include the following:

U.S. badges, patches and tabs
Expert Infantryman Badge
Combat Action Badge
Master Parachutist Badge (United States)
Air Assault Badge
Army Staff Identification Badge
Office of the Joint Chiefs of Staff Identification Badge
 Ranger tab
101st Airborne Division Shoulder Sleeve Insignia worn as his Combat Service Identification Badge
101st Airborne Division Distinctive Unit Insignia
11 Overseas Service Bars
Foreign badges
British Army Parachutist Badge
Basic French Parachutist Badge (French: *Brevet de Parachutisme militaire*)

German Parachutist Badge in bronze

(German: *Fallschirmspringerabzeichen*)

 German Armed Forces Badge for Military Proficiency Bronze

U.S. military decorations

Defense Distinguished Service Medal (with 3 Oak Leaf Clusters)

Distinguished Service Medal (with 2 Oak Leaf Clusters)

Defense Superior Service Medal (with Oak Leaf Cluster)

Legion of Merit (with 3 Oak Leaf Clusters)

 Bronze Star (with V Device)

Defense Meritorious Service Medal

Meritorious Service Medal (with 2 Oak Leaf Clusters)

 Joint Service Commendation Medal

Army Commendation Medal (with 2 Oak Leaf Clusters)

 Joint Service Achievement Medal

Army Achievement Medal

U.S. unit awards

Joint Meritorious Unit Award (with 3 Oak Leaf Clusters)

Army Meritorious Unit Commendation

Army Superior Unit Award

U.S. non-military decorations

State Department Secretary's Distinguished Service Award

State Department Distinguished Honor Award

State Department Superior Honor Award

U.S. service (campaign) medals and service and training ribbons

National Defense Service Medal (with 2 Service Stars)

Armed Forces Expeditionary Medal (with 2 Service Stars)

Afghanistan Campaign Medal (with 3 Service Stars)

Iraq Campaign Medal (with 4 Service Stars)

Global War on Terrorism Expeditionary Medal

Global War on Terrorism Service Medal

Armed Forces Service Medal

Humanitarian Service Medal

Army Service Ribbon

Army Overseas Service Ribbon (with award numeral 8)

International decorations

United Nations Mission in Haiti (UNMIH) Medal

NATO Meritorious Service Medal Iraq & Afghanistan with bronze service star

NATO Medal for Yugoslavia, NTM-I, Afghanistan with 2 bronze service stars

Foreign state decorations
Honorary Officer of the Order of Australia, Military Division
Meritorious Service Cross, Military Division (Canada)
Cross of Merit of the Minister of Defence of the Czech Republic, 1st Grade
Commander of the Legion of Honour (France)
French Military Campaign Medal
Grand Officer's Cross of the Order of Merit of the Federal Republic of Germany
Gold Award of the Iraqi Order of the Date Palm
Gold Cross of Merit of the Carabinieri (Italy)
Order of National Security Merit, Tong-il Security Medal (Korea)
Knight Grand Cross with Swords of the Order of Orange-Nassau (Netherlands)
Commander of the Order of Merit of the Republic of Poland
Polish Iraq Star
Polish Army Medal, Gold
Romanian Chief of Defense Honor Emblem
Military Merit Order, First Class (United Arab Emirates)

Honorary degrees

Eckerd College, May 23, 2010, honorary doctorate in laws

University of Pennsylvania, May 14, 2012, honorary doctorate of laws

Dickinson College, May 20, 2012, honorary doctorate of public service

Additional recognitions

In 2007, *Time* named Petraeus one of the 100 most influential leaders and revolutionaries of the year as well as one of its four runners up for Time Person of the Year.

He was also named the second most influential American conservative by *The Daily Telegraph* as well as *The Daily Telegraph*'s 2007 Man of the Year. In 2005, Petraeus was identified as one of America's top leaders by *U.S. News & World Report*.

In 2008, a poll conducted by *Foreign Policy* and *Prospect* magazines selected Petraeus as one of the world's top 100 public intellectuals. Also in 2008, the Static Line Association named Petraeus as its 2008 Airborne Man of the Year, and *Der Spiegel* named him "America's most respected soldier."

As 2008 came to a close, *Newsweek* named him the 16th most powerful person in the world in its December 20, 2008, edition, and *Prospect* magazine named him the "Public Intellectual of the

Year". He was also named as one of the "75 Best People in the World" in the October 2009 issue of *Esquire*,

The OSS Society awarded Petraeus its Donovan Award May 2, 2009. In his introduction of Petraeus, Maj. Gen. John K. Singlub, USA, Ret., a 2007 award recipient and OSS Society chairman, said "The William J. Donovan Award is given to an individual who has rendered distinguished service in the interests of the democratic process, public service, courage in all its forms and the cause of freedom." The National Committee on American Foreign Policy (NCAFP) during its 35th Anniversary Gala and Award Dinner on May 28, 2009 in New York City, presented the George F. Kennan Award for Distinguished Public Service to Petraeus. The American Legion awarded its highest honor, the Distinguished Service Medal on August 25, 2009 at its 91st National Convention in Louisville, Kentucky.

On February 20, 2010, Petraeus received Princeton University's Madison Medal, named after the fourth president of the United States, who many consider to be Princeton's first graduate student. Established by the Association of Princeton Graduate Alumni, it is presented each year by the University to an alumnus or alumna of the Graduate School who has had a distinguished career, advanced the cause of graduate education or achieved an outstanding record of public service. May 27, 2010, The Intrepid Sea, Air & Space Museum awarded its Freedom Award to Petraeus. "The Intrepid Museum's mission is to honor the men and women who have served our nation. General Petraeus has led our troops overseas in that exact effort, and we are indebted to his leadership and love of country", said Susan Marenoff, Executive Director of the Intrepid Sea, Air & Space Museum. "This annual event throws a spotlight on individuals who have gone above and beyond the call of duty for our nation." On September 20, the American Political Science Association (APSA) presented Petraeus with its 2010 Hubert H. Humphrey Award in recognition of notable public service by a political scientist.

On December 9, 2010, Barbara Walters picked Petraeus for the Most Fascinating Person of 2010. Walters called the top commander in Afghanistan "an American hero". Petraeus was chosen as "one of Time magazine's 50 "People Who Mattered" in December 2010.

The same year he was named number 12 of 50 people who mattered in 2010 by the *New Statesmen* magazine, and Petraeus was listed as number 8 of 100 Foreign Policy Top 100 Global Thinkers for 2011.

Early January 2011, Pete Hegseth and Wade Zirkle from Vets for Freedom, wrote an Op-Ed for the *Wall Street Journal* making a claim that Petraeus should be promoted to Five-Star which would make him General of the Army. In April, Petraeus was named in the 2011 Time 100. The Institute for the Study of War, 2011, National Security Leadership Award was presented to Petraeus on August 4, 2011. The New Statesman annual survey presents the most influential people from pop stars and dissident activists to tech gurus and heads of state, the people doing most to shape our world keep changing. September 26, 2011, Petraeus was listed as number 2 of the 50 for 2011.

The Association of Special Operations Professionals named Petraeus as its 2011 Man of the Year for 2011, and was presented the award at Ft. Bragg on November 2, 2011 at its annual Special Operations Exposition.

Early January 2012, Petraeus was named one of "The 50 Most Powerful People in Washington" by *GQ magazine*. Petraeus was inducted January 29, 2012, into the Reserve Officers Association's (ROA) Minuteman Hall of Fame as the 2011 Inductee during the 2012 ROA National Security Symposium.

The German Order of Merit was presented to Petraeus February 14, by the German Secretary of Defense Thomas de Maizière. According to de Maizière, he is an "outstanding strategist and a true friend of the German people." On March 16, 2012, the Dutch Minister of Defense Hans Hillen knighted Petraeus at the Hague with the Knight Grand Cross of the Order of Orange Nassau with swords. The Minister thanked Petraeus in his speech for his, "unconditional support to the Dutch troops and for being a driving force behind a successful mission. Through his personal efforts for cooperation between the Netherlands and America, the Netherlands could achieve significant operational successes with the Task Force Uruzgan."

Letters from Abbottabad

Captured correspondence from Osama Bin Laden "Letters from Abbottabad" revealed that in May 2010, Bin Laden wanted to target President Barack Obama and General Petraeus, "The reason for concentrating on them is that Obama is the head of infidelity and killing him automatically will make Biden take over the presidency for the remainder of the term, as it is the norm over there. Biden is totally unprepared for that post, which will lead the U.S. into a crisis." It further went on to say, "As for Petraeus, he is the man of the hour in this last year of the war, and killing him would alter the war's path."

Holly Petraeus

General George W. Casey, Jr. presents an award to Petraeus' wife, Holly, in 2007.

The Command and General Staff College Foundation's 2012 Distinguished Leadership Award was presented to Petraeus on May 10, 2012. Petraeus was a recipient of the 2012 Jefferson Award for Public Service, which was presented on June 19, 2012, at a Washington D.C luncheon. The Daughters of the American Revolution (DAR) presented Petraeus with its Patriot Award during the 121st Continental Congress held in DAR Constitution Hall. Petraeus was the keynote speaker during Defense Night when the award was presented. The International Relations Council in Kansas City, MO, presented the Distinguished Service Award for International Statesmanship to Petraeus on September 10, 2012, in Kansas City during its 2012 Annual Awards Banquet. As part of the CIA's 65th birthday, Petraeus visited the New York Stock Exchange and was invited to ring The Opening Bell to commemorate the 65th anniversary of the CIA. The Soldiers', Sailors', Marines', Coast Guard and Airmans' Club presented Petraeus the 2012 Service to the Nation Award at its October 5 Military Ball.

The Royal United Services Institute (RUSI) presented Petraeus with the Chesney Gold Medal on June 10, 2013. The award marks a lifelong distinguished contribution in the defense and international security fields, to the benefit of the United Kingdom and/or the international community. The Jagello 2000 Association for Euro-Atlantic Cooperation from the Czech Republic and the Slovak Atlantic Commission awarded Petraeus the 2013 Czech and Slovak Transatlantic Award September 20, 2013.

David Petraeus' wife, Holly, has been recognized on multiple occasions for her lifelong commitment to supporting military families.

In popular culture

In the 2012 video game Call of Duty: Black Ops 2, Petraeus is portrayed, by a voice actor, as the Secretary of Defense in 2025. Petraeus resigned four days before the game was released.

Works by David Petraeus

Speeches and public remarks

"Institutionalizing Change: Transformation in the US Army, 2005–2007," May 2010.

National Committee on American Foreign Policy George F. Kennan Award Acceptance Remarks. *American Foreign Policy Interests*, July/August 2009, 31(4).

"The Foreign Policy Interview with Gen. David H. Petraeus," January/February 2009.

Small Wars Journal Interview with General David H. Petraeus,"

Published works by David Petraeus

Lorenz, G. C.; Willbanks, James H.; Petraeus, David H.; Stuart, Paul A.; Crittenden, Burr L.; George, Dewey P. (1983). *Operation Junction City, Vietnam 1967 : battle book*. Ft.

Leavenworth, KS: United States Army Command and General Staff College, Combat Studies Institute. OCLC 15637627. DTIC ADA139612

Petraeus, David H. (1983). "What is Wrong with a Nuclear Freeze," Military Review v.63:49–64, November 1983.

Petraeus, David H. (1984). "Light Infantry in Europe: Strategic Flexibility and Conventional Deterrence," Military Review v.64:33–55, December 1984.

Petraeus, David H. (1985). "Review of Richard A. Gabriel's *The Antagonists: A Comparative Combat Assessment of the Soviet and American Soldier*". *Military Affairs* (Lexington, VA: Society for Military History, published January 1985) **49** (1): 17–22. doi:10.2307/1988272. JSTOR 1988272. OCLC 37032240.

Petraeus, David H. (1986), "Lessons of history and lessons of Vietnam", Parameters (Carlisle, PA: US Army War College) 16(3): 43–53, Autumn 1986.

Petraeus, David H. (1987). *The American military and the lessons of Vietnam: a study of military influence and the use of force in the post-Vietnam era*. Princeton, NJ: Princeton University. OCLC 20673428.

Clark, Asa A., Kaufman, Daniel J., and Petraeus, David H. (1987). "Why an Army?" Army Magazine v38(2)26–34, February 1987.

Petraeus, David H. (1987). "El Salvador and the Vietnam Analogy", Armed Force Journal International, February 1987.

Taylor, William J., Jr.; Petraeus, David H. (1987). "The legacy of Vietnam for the U.S. military". In Osborn, George K. *Democracy, strategy, and Vietnam : implications for American policy making*. Lexington, MA: Lexington Books. ISBN 978-0-669-16340-7. OCLC 15518468.

Petraeus, David H. (1987). "Korea, the Never-Again Club, and Indochina". *Parameters* **17** (4) (Carlisle, PA: U.S. Army War College, published December 1987). pp. 59–70. ISSN 0031-1723. OCLC 1039883. SuDoc No. D 101.72:17/4, GPO Item No. 0325-K, PURL LPS1511.

Golden, James R.; Kaufman, Daniel J.; Clark, Asa A.; Petraeus, David H. (Eds)(1989),"*NATO at Forty: Change Continuity, & Prospects*". Westview Pr.

Petraeus, David H. (1989). "Military Influence And the Post-Vietnam Use of Force". *Armed Forces & Society* (Piscataway, NJ: SAGE Publications, published Summer 1989) **15** (4): 489–505. doi:10.1177/0095327X8901500402. OCLC 49621350.

Petraeus, David H.; Brennan, Robert A. (1997). "Walk and Shoot Training". *Infantry Magazine* **87** (1) (Ft. Benning, GA: U.S. Army Infantry School, published January–February 1997). pp. 36–40. Retrieved August 10, 2011.

Petraeus, David H.; Carr, Damian P.; Abercrombie, John C. (1997). "Why We Need FISTs—Never Send a Man When You Can Send a Bullet" (PDF). *Field Artillery* **1997** (3) (Fort Sill, OK: US Army Field Artillery School, published May–June 1997). pp. 3–5. ISSN 0899-2525. OCLC 16516511. HQDA PB6-97-3, USPS 309-010, PURL LPS13201, SuDoc No. D 101.77/2: 1997/3. Retrieved August 26, 2007.

"Lessons of the Iraq War and Its Aftermath". Washington Institute for Near East Policy. 2004.

(2006) "Learning Counterinsurgency: Observations from Soldiering in Iraq," *Military Review*

Petraeus, David H. (2006). "A Conversation with Lieutenant General David H. Petraeus". *Insights* **3** (1) (Suffolk, VA: Lockheed Martin, published March 2006). pp. 2–5, 28–29.

(2007) The US Army/Marine Corps Counterinsurgency Field Manual (Forward)"FM-3-24"

(2007) "Beyond the Cloister," *The American Interest Magazine*

Petraeus, David H. (2007). "Iraq: Progress in the Face of Challenge". *Army Magazine* **57** (10) (Arlington, VA: Association of the US Army, published October 2007). pp. 115–123.

Petraeus, David H. (2010). "Counterinsurgency Concepts: What We Learned in Iraq". *Global Policy* **1** (1): 116–117. doi:10.1111/j.1758-5899.2009.00003.x.

Petraeus, David H. (2010) "Shoulder to shoulder in Afghanistan", *Policy Options*, April 2010.

Petraeus, David H. (2011). "Ryan C. Crocker: Diplomat and Partner Extraordinaire". *Army Magazine* **61** (4) (Arlington, VA: Association of the US Army, published April 2011). pp. 16, 18.

Petraeus, David H. (2012). "CIA's Directorate of Science and Technology, In-Q-Tel, and the Private Sector". *Intelligencer: Journal of U.S. Intelligence Studies* (Falls Church, VA: Association of Former Intelligence Officers, published Summer-Fall 2012). pp. 7–10.

Petraeus, David H.; Goodfriend, Sydney E. (2013). "Training Veterans for Their Next Mission". *Wall Street Journal* (New York City, NY: Wall Street Journal, published March 26, 2013).

Petraeus, David H.; O'Hanlon, Michael (2013). "An American future filled with promise". *Washington Post* (Washington, D.C.: Washington Post, published April 7, 2013).

Petraeus, David H.; O'Hanlon, Michael (2013). "Fund - don't cut U.S. soft power". *Politico* (Arlington, VA: Politico, published April 30, 2013).

Bremmer, Ian; Petraeus, David (2013). "Abe's electoral win is great news for Japan". *Financial Times* (July 22, 2013).

Petraeus, David; O'Hanlon, Michael (2013). "Petraeus and O'Hanlon: Compromise on budget". *USA Today* (August 4, 2013).

Petraeus, David H. (2013). "Reflections on the Counter-Insurgency Era". *RUSI Journal* (August 14, 2013).

Petraeus, David; O'Hanlon, Michael (2013). "The success story next door". *Politico* (September 24, 2013).

Petraeus, David H. (2013). "How we won in Iraq: And why all the hard-won gains of the surge are in grave danger of being lost today". *Foreign Policy* (October 29, 2013).

In Closing…..

As we look back on the career of General David Petraeus, some may see a soldier that served his country honorably and left the footprint of America all over this globe.

Others may see a failure of a man who lost all respect, when he had an affair that ultimately tarnished his reputation.

But for every person whose lives are better today, because David Petraeus was there to make a difference in their time of need, "He will always be remembered as a HERO"

Today the United States Military is full of soldiers striving to

"Walk in the footsteps of a hero"

A great man once said:

So when they continued asking him, he lifted up himself, and said unto them,

"He that is without sin among you, let him first cast a stone at her".

John 8:7 King James Version (KJV)

Look for these and other great books By David Pietras

From "Mommy to Monster"

The "Daddy Dearest" Club

The Manson Family "Then and Now"

When Love Kills

The Making of a Nightmare

THE INFAMOUS "FLORIDA 5"

Death, Murder, and Vampires Real Vampire Stories

The Life and Death of Richard Ramirez, The Night Stalker (History's Killers Unmasked Series)

Profiling The Killer of a Childhood Beauty Queen

No Justice For Caylee Anthony

A Texas Style Witch Hunt "Justice Denied" The Darlie Lynn Routier Story by

The Book of Revelations Explained The End Times

Murder of a Childhood

John Gotti: A True Mafia Don (History's Killers Unmasked Series)

MURDERED FOR HIS MILLIONS The Abraham Shakespeare Case

The Son of Sam "Then and Now" The David Berkowitz Story

A LOOK INSIDE THE FIVE MAFIA FAMILIES OF NEW YORK CITY

Unmasking The Real Hannibal Lecter

Top 10 Most Haunted Places in America

40 minutes in Abbottabad The Raid on Osama bin Laden

In The Footsteps of a Hero The Military Journey of General David H. Petraeus

BATTLEFIELD BENGHAZI

CASE CLOSED The State of Florida vs. George Zimmerman THE TRUTH REVEALED

CROSSING THE THIN BLUE LINE

THE GHOST FROM MY CHILDHOOD A TRUE GHOST STORY ABOUT THE GELSTON CASTLE AND THE GHOST OF "AUNT" HARRIET DOUGLAS...

Haunted United Kingdom

In Search of Jack the Ripper (History's Killers Unmasked Series)

The Last Ride of Bonnie and Clyde

The Meaning of a Tragedy Canada's Serial Killers Revealed

MOMSTER

Murder In The Kingdom

The Shroud of Turin and the Mystery Surrounding Its Authenticity

The Unexplained World That We Live In

Made in the USA
Las Vegas, NV
02 March 2022